Citrus

SWEET & SAVORY
SUN-KISSED RECIPES

VALERIE AIKMAN-SMITH
& VICTORIA PEARSON

TEN SPEED PRESS
BERKELEY

Contents

Dishes by Course

Breakfast

Blueberry Ricotta Pancakes
with Lemon Cream 4

Lemony Breakfast Eggs 7

Tropical Granola with Candied Lime 35

Breakfast Crepes with
Candied Tangerines 99

Burnt Cinnamon-Sugar
Grapefruit 129

Dark Chocolate Waffles
with Maple Kumquats 153

Starters

Gravadlax with Lemons &
Green Peppercorns 11

Farmhouse Ricotta with
Persian Lime Oil 36

Halibut Ceviche with
Lime & Tequila 39

Halloumi with Preserved Lime,
Cucumber & Mint Salsa 40

Lime & Chile Salted Almonds 52

Moroccan Flatbread 100

Crudités with Pomelo Aioli 130

Mains

Whole Roasted Fish with Lemon
& Fennel Flowers 14

Salt-Crusted Cornish Hens
with Lemon Butter 17

Pork Chops with Eureka
Lemon Mustard 18

Handmade Lemon Pappardelle 20

Linguine with Clams & Lime 43

Lime Chicken Curry 44

Dungeness Crab with Lime
& Chile Dipping Sauce 45

Grilled Sardines with Orange
& Polenta 67

Osso Buco with Orange
Gremolata 68

Panfried Scallops with Smoky
Jalapeño & Tangerine Relish 104

Grilled Honey Mandarin
Chicken Drumettes 105

Tangerine Sticky Ribs 107

Prosciutto Roasted Pork Loin
Stuffed with Grapefruit 136

Scallops with Oroblanco Cream 137

Yuzu-Glazed Salmon 148

Grilled Duck with Ginger Kumquats 150

Salads, Soups & Sides

Meyer Lemon & Thyme
Hearth Bread 8

Lebanese Lentil & Lemon Soup 12

Roasted Salmon Salad with Anchovy
& Lemon Dressing 13

Greek Lemon Herbed Potatoes 19

Cara Cara & Blood Orange Salad with
Ricotta Salata 64

Honey Oranges with Lavender
Flowers 80

Fennel, Tangerine & Olive Slaw 103

Szechuan Shrimp & Ruby
Grapefruit Salad 133

Yellow Grapefruit & Avocado Salad 134

Citrus Japanese Rice 151

Desserts

Lemon Gâteau 22

Burnt Sugar Meyer Lemon Tart 25

Turkish Yogurt Cake with Lime
Syrup & Pistachios 46

Coconut Rice Pudding with
Makrut Limes 49

Key Lime Pie 51

Earl Grey Poached Pears 73

Orange & Rosemary Polenta Cake 75

Orange Blossom Macarons 76

Bergamot Panna Cotta 79

Honey Oranges with Lavender Flowers 80

Valencia Orange Bread &
Butter Pudding 83

Candied Chocolate Mandarins 111

Mandarin Meringue Tart 112

Satsumas in Sweet Wine 115

Burnt Cinnamon-Sugar Grapefruit 129

Pomelo & Basil Granita 139

Pomelo Possets with Candied Peel 140

Dark Chocolate Waffles
with Maple Kumquats 153

Stripy Citrus Pops 166

Drinks

Rosemary Lemonade 26

Limoncello 29

Lime & Coconut Lassi 55

Havana Mojito 56

Orange Blossom Almond Milk 84

Bergamot & Mint Tisane 89

Icy Blood Orange Margarita 90

Orange Wedding Wine 93

Tangerine Daiquiri 117

Page Tangerine Negroni 119

Yuzu Cocktail 157

Pantry Staples

Preserved Limes 54

Orange & Campari Marmalade 71

Orange Bitters 87

Clementine Curd 108

Preserved Tangerines 116

Grapefruit & Gin Marmalade 125

Kumquat Butter 147

Candied Citron 154

Citrus Salt 158

Citrus Oil 161

Citrus Crisps 162

Candied Peel 165

Introduction

Citrus bursts onto the winter scene just after the last of the beautiful fall fruits have faded, brightening and scenting the gray winter months. Like jewels, they remind us of rays of sunshine from which they have been growing and ripening throughout the summer.

It was on one of these winter days that Victoria called and said she was harvesting citrus from her garden and didn't know what to do with it all. She asked if there was a citrus cookbook I could recommend. "Why don't we write one!" I suggested. And *Citrus* was born. What could be better than to work on a book with Victoria; plus it was a good excuse to drive to Ojai and shoot at her studio in amongst the heavenly citrus groves.

Under the watchful eye of the Topa Topa Mountains in Ojai—nestled in among the colorful floral citrus groves—is Victoria's house. Pixies, Kishus, oranges, grapefruits, and all things citrus ripen in the groves all year round. In March, when the blossoms explode, the air is filled with an unforgettable heady, hypnotic perfume, which lingers long into the evening. If Victoria has been away on location for a few days, the house will trap and concentrate the citrus blossom scents. When she returns home and opens the door, she is hit by the magical perfume.

Victoria inherited oranges, lemons, grapefruit, and a mystery citrus from the previous owners, so there is an endless supply year round—the envy of Midwest and East Coast friends and family. This made her realize just how lucky she was to be able to pop outside and pluck a fat juicy lemon off one of her trees to squeeze over a salad. Her canning skills come in handy when she needs to make marmalades with all the bounty. Orange

blossoms churn up teenage memories of driving in her parents' 1965 Mustang with the top down on a warm California evening, the air heavy with scent. In fact, oranges were center stage at her wedding: swags of orange leaves and fruit adorned the rustic gate to welcome guests, and the cake was decorated with perfect marzipan oranges, leaves, and blossoms. She even made *vin d'orange* (see page 93) for her wedding, which was bottled the night before by friends and family.

I live in Los Angeles with a garden that can only sustain cactus, but I have six large pots, which I proudly call "my grove," where lemons, kumquats, and makrut limes all nestle together under the hot California sun. They are pollinated by bees and brightly colored humming birds—a wonderful bonus. When they bloom, the air is floral, even with only six pots. My love for citrus grew as soon I moved to Los Angeles; everywhere I looked there were trees laden with lemons, oranges, grapefruits, and limes. Californians are so used to this that they leave fallen fruit on the ground. How could this be? The cook in me would go around and gather all this forgotten fruit and make jams and marmalades. Then I started to expand my repertoire, leaning heavily on Spanish and North African influences, lacing dishes with preserved lemons and perfuming them with orange blossoms. I began to dry orange peel to go in Szechuan recipes, salts, and sugars. I love to mix and match the wonderful bright zest and tangy flavors with heady spices and freshly picked herbs, marrying it all to Californian produce.

When I was a child growing up in Scotland, one of the highlights of Christmas was finding a bright orange tangerine at the bottom of my stocking—a magical treat in itself. The fruits had come from warm sunny climates far from the snowy dark winter of Scotland. I never dreamed that one day I would live in one of the most abundant citrus states and cook with such wonderful fruits.

One of my favorite things to do is visit local farms where I can pick my own fruit. Walking through the quiet groves with bees buzzing in the air and trees laden with juicy plump fruits makes me appreciate where the fruit has come from. You get to experience the real farm-to-table taste. I come home revitalized, my head exploding with ideas of what I am going to create with this wonderful plunder.

We've brought our love for all things citrus in the following chapters through personal recipes that we love to cook. Talking to local growers and sellers at our farmers' markets yields a goldmine of knowledge and tips and is a nice way to share recipes and ideas. We encourage everyone to look for the lesser known varieties of citrus and have fun discovering new flavors.

But most of all, be mindful when you eat your next orange. Take time to peel it with care, smell the fragrance, and think about the star-shaped blossoms that soaked up the sun and rain to create this citrus wonder. And then enjoy every last bite.

—VALERIE AIKMAN-SMITH

Citrus Basics

Citrus fruits are easy to work with, requiring only the simplest preparation techniques. Here are a handful of basic tips to help you select, store, and prepare them. If you already have a favored way of handling these everyday tasks, skip this page and go right into the kitchen.

Buying Citrus

If possible, visit a local pick-your-own citrus orchard, where you will typically get the freshest and brightest-tasting fruit. Alternatively, try to shop at farmers' markets and grocery stores that carry regionally cultivated fruits, as citrus from out of state or out of the country is picked unripe for transport. If you do not live in a citrus-growing area, seek out purveyors who take care in selecting the fruits they stock.

In general, look for citrus fruits that are heavy for their size; firm; free of soft spots, wrinkles, or bruises; and show no signs of puffiness. Although good color is appealing, it does not always indicate ripeness or quality.

Storing Citrus

Store fruits in a cool, dry, dark place, where they will stay fresh for a few days. They will keep in the refrigerator for even longer—up to two to three weeks. Avoid putting them in sealed plastic bags, as they will soften more quickly and may mold. You can also freeze the juice for up to 6 months.

Zesting Citrus

Rinse and dry the fruit well. If you will be both zesting and juicing the fruit, always remove the zest first. To finely grate the zest, use a rasp-type grater, such as a Microplane, or the smallest holes on a box grater, being careful to remove only the colored portion of the peel and not the white pith directly beneath it. To remove the zest in strips, use a razor-sharp vegetable peeler, again being careful to remove only the colored portion of the peel.

Juicing Citrus

First, roll the citrus fruit firmly on a work surface or squeeze it between your palms. This will bruise the interior cells that hold the juice so that it will release more easily. Cut the fruit in half crosswise. Then, holding a citrus half over a bowl, stick a citrus reamer into the center of the cut side and turn and squeeze the citrus half to release the juice into the bowl. A citrus press or a juicer can also be used and is a time-saver when larger amounts of juice are needed.

Peeling and Segmenting Citrus

Most citrus fruits can be peeled by simply starting near the stem end and pulling the peel away with your fingers. Or, cut off a thin slice from the stem end, score the fruit into quarters through the peel, and then pull the peel away.

To peel a citrus fruit so that it is free of all pith, using a sharp knife, cut a thin slice off both ends of the fruit to make a flat surface and stand the fruit upright. Then, following the curve of the fruit, cut downward to remove the peel and white pith, rotating the fruit as you work until all of the peel and pith is cut away.

The fruit can now be sliced or cut into pieces. To supreme the citrus, hold the peeled fruit in your hand over a bowl and, using a sharp knife, cut along both sides of each segment to free it from the membrane, catching the segments and any juice in the bowl.

Lemon

Lemon

The lemons you find at farmers' markets have been plucked ripe from the trees the day before their journey. Tree-ripened in lush, perfumed groves under the hot sun, the sound of bees buzzing in the air, the fruits arrive plump and firm, with shiny skins and juicy interiors. In urban California, lemon trees—both cultivated and rogue—are everywhere, spilling over neighborhood rickety fences and lining sidewalks in commercial stretches. You can literally walk around your block and pick all the lemons you want. For those who live in cooler climates, you can find lemons at any supermarket and most corner stores.

Lemons are a kitchen staple. Keep a handful around all the time and you'll quickly see how often you use them in both sweet and savory recipes. And if you are feeling a little under the weather, a hot toddy—whiskey, honey, water, and lemon juice—is guaranteed to make you feel better. Plus, you can use lemon juice to clean your silverware and silver jewelry, brass and copper, and to remove stains from clothing. And once you have zested, peeled, and juiced your lemon and you are down to the bare bones, just pop it down your waste disposal. It will not only disinfect it but also refresh it with a bright, lemony smell.

The no-frills *Eureka lemon* is the most commonly available lemon, used in every kitchen and sold in nearly every grocery store year-round. It has a pleasantly tart flavor and a thick skin, which makes it excellent for preserving. Freshly cut Eureka wedges are ideal for squeezing over grilled fish, and the juice and zest make both the Lemon Gâteau (page 22) and the Lebanese Lentil & Lemon Soup (page 12) sing. The *Lisbon lemon* is similar to the Eureka, but with a slightly tarter flavor. Either variety can be used in any of the recipes in this chapter.

The *Meyer lemon*, a cross between a lemon and an orange or a mandarin (its paternity remains unsettled), has thin skin, a unique floral scent, and a sweet, fragrant taste. Less acidic than the Eureka or the Lisbon, the Meyer is great in drinks, sorbets, ice creams, and syrups. The round *Persian lemon*, also known as Persian sweet lemon, looks like a Meyer, has greenish flesh, and is as sweet as an orange. It is found mostly in gardens and small orchards in Southern California and, unlike other lemons, is delicious eaten out of hand.

The *Pink Lemonade lemon*, also known as Variegated Pink-Fleshed Eureka lemon, has green-and-cream-striped skin when young and lovely pink flesh, which makes it a particularly pretty drink garnish. As this lemon matures, it loses its stripes and the color of its flesh intensifies. It is fun to swap these for regular Eureka lemons, as you will get the same taste but a bolder color.

The *Ponderosa lemon*, which is likely a cross between a lemon and a citron, can weigh up to four pounds and typically has lots of seeds. Its hardy skin makes the fruit ideal for marmalade. It's usually available only at farmers' markets, most often from a citrus grower who likes to experiment with the entire citrus spectrum.

This chapter includes some imaginative recipes for using lemons, from a thirst-quenching Rosemary Lemonade (page 26) and light, easy poached eggs with a lemony yogurt sauce (page 7) to lemon-scented handmade pappardelle (page 20). Indeed, you may find yourself cooking with this versatile citrus so much that you'll end up planting a lemon tree or two in your yard.

Lemon-infused ricotta pancakes are a must for us, especially at the height of lemon season. We have made them with Eureka lemons as well as Meyer lemons, and both are equally heavenly.

BLUEBERRY RICOTTA PANCAKES WITH LEMON CREAM

~Serves 6

1 cup all-purpose flour

1 teaspoon baking powder

$1/3$ cup light brown sugar

2 eggs

$1/2$ cup whole milk

$1^{1}/_{2}$ cups whole-milk ricotta cheese

Zest and juice of 1 lemon

1 cup fresh blueberries

$1/2$ tablespoon unsalted butter

Confectioners' sugar, for dusting

LEMON CREAM

1 (8-ounce) tub mascarpone

Zest and juice of 1 lemon

To make the batter, place the flour, baking powder, brown sugar, eggs, milk, ricotta, and lemon zest and juice into a blender and blend until smooth.

Pour half of the blueberries into a bowl and mash with a fork until broken up. Pour in the batter and mix to combine.

To make the lemon cream, in a bowl, whisk together the mascarpone with the lemon zest and juice. Set aside.

Place a large frying pan over medium heat. When the pan is hot, add the butter and swirl the pan to coat the bottom evenly.

Working in batches, for each pancake pour $1/4$ cup of the batter into the pan. Cook until small bubbles appear on the surface and the bottom is golden, about 2 minutes. Using a spatula, flip the pancakes and cook until golden brown and cooked through.

Arrange the pancakes on a warm platter and cover with a kitchen towel to keep warm while you finish the rest.

Toss the remaining blueberries into the hot pan and cook until warmed through, about 1 minute. To serve, sprinkle the pancakes with the blueberries and dust with the confectioners' sugar. Serve the lemon cream on the side.

Here's a twist on eggs Benedict, and a simpler, lighter way to start the day. You can make the sauce the night before, freeing you up in the morning to poach the eggs. Eureka lemons impart a tart, bright taste that livens up this dish.

LEMONY BREAKFAST EGGS

~Serves 4

SAUCE

1 cup plain Greek yogurt

Zest and juice of 1 Eureka lemon

2 tablespoons chopped fresh dill

2 English muffins, split

8 slices smoked salmon

1 teaspoon freshly squeezed lemon juice

4 eggs

Sea salt and freshly cracked black pepper

Dill sprigs, for garnish

Eureka lemon wedges, for serving

To make the sauce, whisk together in a small bowl the yogurt, lemon zest and juice, and dill, mixing well. Cover and refrigerate until ready to use or for up to 1 day.

Toast the muffin halves and place on 4 plates. Spoon a little lemon sauce on each muffin half and top with 2 salmon slices.

To poach the eggs, fill a medium saucepan two-thirds full with water and bring to a simmer over medium heat. Add the lemon juice. Crack 1 egg into a ramekin or a small bowl. Whisk the water to create a vortex, and gently pour the egg into the spinning water. Repeat with the remaining 3 eggs, one at a time, and gently simmer for 2 to 3 minutes. Using a slotted spoon, remove the eggs, shake off any excess water, and place on top of the salmon.

Spoon more of the yogurt sauce over each egg, sprinkle with salt and pepper and garnish with the dill. Serve immediately, with the lemon wedges on the side.

Juicy Meyer lemons and freshly picked lemon thyme add a perfumed, zesty kick to this simple, no-nonsense focaccia. It will surely become part of your life very quickly.

MEYER LEMON & THYME HEARTH BREAD

~Serves 6 to 8

1 cup warm water
(about 110 °F)

¼ cup olive oil

1 package (¼ ounce/
7 grams) active dry yeast

3 cups unbleached
all-purpose flour

1 teaspoon fine sea salt

4 Meyer lemons, thinly
sliced

1 small bunch lemon thyme

Coarse sea salt, for
sprinkling

Pour the water into a measuring jug, stir in the oil, and sprinkle the yeast over the top. Let stand for about 5 minutes, until frothy.

Place the flour and salt in a food processor and pulse until mixed. Then, with the motor running, add the yeast mixture to the flour and process for about 4 minutes, until the dough comes together and forms a ball. Transfer the dough to an oiled bowl and turn to coat on all sides. Cover with plastic wrap, set aside in a warm place, and let the dough rise for about 1½ hours, until it doubles in size.

Oil a 9 by 13-inch sheet pan. Transfer the dough to the center of the prepared sheet pan, punching it down to deflate it. Then, using your fingers, press and stretch the dough out evenly in the pan, extending it to the edges. Using your fingertips, dimple the entire surface of the dough. Cover with plastic wrap and set aside for 30 minutes. Meanwhile, preheat the oven to 375°F.

Uncover the dough, arrange the lemon slices on top and scatter with the lemon thyme. Sprinkle generously with the coarse sea salt.

Bake for 25 to 30 minutes, until golden brown. Serve warm.

Thinly sliced and served on bread topped with capers and wafer-thin red onions, gravadlax is an absolute crowd pleaser. The bright taste of the lemon along with the briny green peppercorns makes for a delicate and vibrant salmon cure. Use fresh wild or sustainable farm-raised salmon.

GRAVADLAX WITH LEMONS & GREEN PEPPERCORNS

~Makes about 3 pounds gravadlax

1 (3-pound) skin-on center-cut salmon fillet

1/2 cup firmly packed dark brown sugar

1 cup coarse sea salt

2 tablespoons brined green peppercorns

2 lemons, thinly sliced

1/4 cup vodka

Place the salmon, skin side down, on a work surface. Run your fingers down its length to check for pin bones, removing any you find with kitchen pliers. Cut the fillet in half crosswise.

Mix together the sugar, salt, and peppercorns in a small bowl. Line the bottom of a deep ceramic or glass baking dish with one-third of the salt mixture and layer half of the lemon slices evenly on top.

Place one piece of the salmon skin side down on top of the salt mixture. Sprinkle with half of the remaining salt and drizzle with the vodka. Place the other piece of salmon on top, flesh side down, and cover evenly with the remaining salt. Top with the rest of the lemon slices.

Cover the dish with plastic wrap, making sure it is airtight. Place a heavy pan or cans on top of the plastic wrap to weigh it down. Refrigerate for 48 hours.

Remove the dish from the refrigerator and remove the weights and plastic wrap. Transfer the salmon to a work surface and, using the back of a knife, scrape off and discard all of the excess salt mixture. Thinly slice and serve.

The cured salmon will keep tightly covered in the refrigerator for up to 5 days.

Tangy lemons infuse this wonderfully thick and comforting soup, which can be found throughout the Middle East with varying ingredients. Lemon, lentils, and spinach, however, are a mainstay. Serve it with Meyer Lemon & Thyme Hearth Bread (page 8) for a delicious supper.

LEBANESE LENTIL & LEMON SOUP

~Serves 4 to 6

2 tablespoons olive oil

1 clove garlic, smashed

1 yellow onion, sliced

1½ cups brown lentils, picked over and rinsed

1 teaspoon ground cumin

1 teaspoon ground coriander

Zest and juice of 3 large lemons

4 cups chicken stock

2 cups baby spinach

Salt and freshly ground black pepper

Plain Greek yogurt, for serving

Ground sumac, for sprinkling

In a large saucepan, heat the oil over medium-high heat. Add the garlic and onion and sauté for about 5 minutes, until translucent and lightly golden. Add the lentils, cumin, coriander, and lemon zest and stir to combine.

Pour in the stock and bring to a boil. Turn down the heat to a gentle simmer and cook, uncovered, for about 30 minutes, until the lentils are tender. Add the lemon juice and spinach and cook for 2 to 3 minutes longer, until the spinach wilts. Remove from the heat, season with salt and pepper.

Pour the soup into a blender and puree. You may want to add a little water if the consistency is too thick.

Ladle into bowls and swirl in some yogurt. Sprinkle with sumac and serve.

This piquant dressing of tart lemon and salty anchovies—a play on the northern Italian anchovy dip *bagna cauda*—turns this everyday salad into something to remember. If you can't find wild salmon, look for sustainable, organic farm-raised salmon.

ROASTED SALMON SALAD WITH ANCHOVY & LEMON DRESSING

~Serves 4

1 (1-pound) skin-on, center-cut wild salmon fillet

Sea salt and freshly cracked black pepper

Large pinch of dried oregano

2 cloves garlic, finely minced

6 anchovy fillets

Zest and juice of 1 small lemon

3 tablespoons extra virgin olive oil

4 cups salad greens

2 shallots, thinly sliced

Preheat the oven to 425°F. Place a cast-iron or heavy sauté pan in the oven for 10 minutes to get it smoking hot.

Season the salmon with salt and pepper and sprinkle with the oregano. Remove the pan from the oven and place the salmon, skin side down, in the pan. Return the pan to the oven and roast for 15 minutes, until the salmon is opaque and cooked through.

While the salmon is cooking, in a blender, place the garlic, anchovies, lemon zest and juice, and oil and process until smooth. Pour into a small saucepan, place over low heat, and warm through.

Remove the salmon from the oven and let rest for 5 minutes. Meanwhile, in a large bowl, toss together the salad greens and shallots, drizzle with the anchovy dressing, and toss to coat evenly.

Using 2 forks, break up the salmon into bite-size pieces and add them to the salad. Season with pepper and serve.

Fennel grows wild all over California, and in the summer, when the bright yellow flowers are in full bloom, whole hillsides come alive. Mixing the flowers with lemons is a perfect union for stuffing fresh fish, and a splash of Pernod, with its heady aniseed taste, deepens the flavors.

WHOLE ROASTED FISH WITH LEMON & FENNEL FLOWERS

~Serves 6 to 8

1 (2- to 3-pound) ocean trout, cleaned

4 lemons, thinly sliced

1 fennel bulb, stalks and fronds removed if still attached and bulb thinly sliced

Handful of fennel flowers

¼ cup extra virgin olive oil

Pernod, for drizzling

Sea salt and freshly cracked black pepper

Preheat the oven to 375°F. Line a sheet pan with parchment paper.

Rinse the fish and pat dry with paper towels. Lay the fish on the prepared pan and stuff the cavity generously with the lemon and fennel slices, reserving a few of the lemon slices. Place the remaining lemon slices and the fennel flowers on top of the fish.

Using butcher's twine, tie the fish at 4 evenly spaced intervals along its length. Drizzle with the oil and top with a few splashes of Pernod. Season with salt and pepper.

Cover the fish with a large piece of parchment paper, tucking the parchment under the fish to form a parcel. Roast for 35 to 40 minutes. To test for doneness, insert a small knife near the backbone; the flesh should be opaque and the juices clear.

When the fish is cooked, remove the parchment and transfer the fish to a platter. Snip and remove the strings, then serve at once.

Cooking the hens in a salt crust leaves them incredibly succulent, allows the zesty lemon butter to infuse the meat, and—believe it or not—doesn't make the chicken salty at all.

SALT-CRUSTED CORNISH HENS WITH LEMON BUTTER

~Serves 4

1/2 cup unsalted butter, at room temperature

Zest and juice of 1 lemon

2 Cornish hens

1 lemon, thinly sliced

4 pounds coarse sea salt

Preheat the oven to 375°F.

In a small bowl, mix together the butter and the lemon zest and juice until well combined.

Put the hens, breast side up, on a work surface. Spread the butter under the skin and on top of the breasts and thighs. Lay the lemon slices on top and inside the birds.

Pour the salt into a large bowl. Slowly add enough water to the salt to create the consistency of wet sand.

Spread a thin layer of the wet salt on the bottom of an ovenproof dish or cast-iron pan large enough to hold the birds. Place the hens on top then cover completely with the remaining salt mixture. Pat the salt securely around the birds to make sure there are no holes that will allow steam to escape.

Roast the hens for 1 hour. The salt will harden and turn golden brown. Remove from the oven and let rest for 10 minutes.

Using the back of a large knife, crack open the crust. Remove the hens and place them on a wooden board. Cut in half lengthwise and serve.

Pork chops make a fast, friendly dinner. Panfried with sharp-flavored Eureka lemons and grainy mustard and finished with freshly picked sage, they're transformed into a feast.

PORK CHOPS WITH EUREKA LEMON MUSTARD

~Serves 2

2 bone-in center-cut pork chops, each about 2 inches thick

¼ cup olive oil

2 tablespoons whole-grain Dijon mustard

Zest and juice of 1 Eureka lemon

Salt and freshly ground black pepper

2 tablespoons torn fresh sage leaves

Put the chops in a single layer in a ceramic or glass dish. In a small bowl, whisk together the oil, mustard, and lemon zest and juice. Season with salt and pepper. Pour the oil mixture over the chops, turn the chops to coat evenly, cover, and refrigerate for at least 2 hours or for up to overnight.

Remove the chops from the refrigerator and bring to room temperature.

Place a sauté pan over high heat until smoking. Remove the chops from the marinade, reserving the marinade, and place the chops in the hot pan. Immediately turn down the heat to medium and cook the chops for 5 minutes. Turn the chops over, pour the reserved marinade into the pan, and toss in the sage leaves. Turn down the heat to low and cook for 5 minutes longer. The chops are ready when they're moist and pale pink in the center.

Lemons and oregano grow all over Greece, and they both play a big part in Mediterranean cuisine. These roasted potatoes come out of the hot oven crispy and infused with the flavors and aromas of the Greek countryside.

GREEK LEMON HERBED POTATOES

~Serves 4

1 pound baby potatoes

Zest and juice of 2 lemons

¼ cup extra virgin olive oil

½ cup loosely packed fresh oregano leaves

Sea salt

Preheat the oven to 425°F.

Put the potatoes in a saucepan, add water to cover by 3 inches, and bring to a boil over high heat. Cook for about 6 minutes, until tender. Drain them and spread the potatoes on a sheet pan. Let cool slightly, then smash each potato with the palm of your hand until flattened but still in one piece.

In a small bowl, whisk together the lemon zest and juice, oil, and oregano and pour the mixture over the potatoes. Toss together, making sure the potatoes are well covered. Generously sprinkle with sea salt.

Roast the potatoes in the preheated oven for 25 to 30 minutes, until browned and crispy. Serve immediately.

Once you've seen how easy it is to make fresh pasta, you'll wonder why you haven't made it before. These rustic noodles need only a splash of excellent olive oil and a dusting of grated Parmesan to make a memorable dinner. You will need a pasta machine, either a hand-cranked model, an electric machine, or one that attaches to a stand mixer.

HANDMADE LEMON PAPPARDELLE

~Serves 6 to 8

3½ cups (1 pound) 00 flour

6 eggs

Zest of 3 lemons

2 tablespoons freshly squeezed lemon juice

Pinch of fine sea salt

In a food processor, combine the flour, eggs, lemon zest and juice, and salt and process until the mixture comes together.

Turn the mixture out onto a floured work surface and knead together for 5 minutes, until smooth. Wrap in plastic wrap and set aside at room temperature for 1 hour.

Cut the dough into 6 equal pieces. Work with 1 piece at a time and keep the remaining pieces covered. Flatten the piece between your palms until it's about ½ inch thick.

Set the rollers of your pasta machine to the widest setting and feed the dough through. Fold the dough in half and repeat on this setting 6 times. Turn the knob of the pasta machine to the next setting and feed the dough through the rollers. Continue to decrease the roller setting after each pass, until the pasta sheet is the desired thickness. Lay the pasta on a lightly floured work surface and cover with a towel. Repeat the process with the remaining dough.

Fold each pasta sheet in half, and then in half again. With a sharp knife, cut the dough into wide strands.

At this point, the pasta is ready to cook. Or, you can freeze the pappardelle in an airtight plastic bag for up to 6 months and then cook straight from the freezer.

To cook and serve the pasta, bring a large pot of water to a boil and add 1 teaspoon of salt. Add the pasta and cook until it floats to the top, about 5 minutes or until al dente.

This simple little cake boasts an immense tart lemon flavor. Dress it up with candied lemon slices or eat it just as it is. Either way, it's a treat.

LEMON GÂTEAU

~Serves 6

⅔ cup unsalted butter, at room temperature

¾ cup granulated sugar

Zest and juice of 3 lemons

2 eggs

¾ cup all-purpose flour

½ teaspoon baking powder

⅔ cup confectioners' sugar

Preheat the oven to 400°F. Butter a 9-inch round springform pan, then dust with flour and tap out the excess.

In the bowl of a stand mixer fitted with the paddle attachment, cream the butter and sugar together on medium speed until light and fluffy. Slowly pour in one-third of the lemon juice, and then add the eggs, one at a time, and continue to beat until well combined. Add the flour and the baking powder and continue to beat until a thick, smooth batter forms. Using a rubber spatula or wooden spoon, fold in two-thirds of the lemon zest until evenly combined. Pour the batter into the prepared pan.

Bake the cake for about 25 minutes, until a thin wooden skewer inserted into the center comes out clean. Transfer to a wire rack and prick the top of the cake all over with the skewer. Set aside.

In a small bowl, whisk together the confectioners' sugar and the remaining lemon zest and juice. Pour the glaze over the cake, and allow to sit for 10 minutes. Remove the cake from the pan, slide it onto a plate, and serve.

Sprinkling sugar over a bright yellow lemon tart and placing it under a searing hot broiler not only results in a mouthwatering dessert but in a beautiful one, too. The caramelized sugar lends crunch and plays well against the sweet tartness of the Meyer lemon.

BURNT SUGAR MEYER LEMON TART

~Serves 6 to 8

Tart Dough (page 112)

3 eggs

4 egg yolks

¼ cup sugar, plus more for dusting

Zest of 4 Meyer lemons

½ cup freshly squeezed Meyer lemon juice

1 cup heavy cream

Prepare the tart dough through to lining the tart pan and chilling for 30 minutes. While the tart shell is chilling, preheat the oven to 375°F.

Remove the tart shell from the refrigerator, uncover, line the bottom with a piece of parchment paper large enough to come up the sides, and fill with pie weights. Bake for 15 minutes, until dry to the touch.

Remove the weights and parchment and bake for another 5 minutes. Transfer the pan to a wire rack and reduce the oven temperature to 325°F.

To make the filling, with an electric handheld mixer, whisk together the eggs, egg yolks, sugar, lemon zest and juice, and cream on medium speed until completely combined. Pour the filling into the tart shell and bake for 25 minutes, until set.

Remove from the oven and turn the oven to broil. Generously sprinkle the top of the tart with sugar, then place under the broiler until the sugar is caramelized.

Let the tart cool on a wire rack. To serve, remove the tart from the pan, transfer it to a large plate, and cut into wedges.

Make a large pitcher of this delicious and refreshing lemonade for a hot summer's day—it's the ideal drink for a backyard barbecue or a children's party. Rub the rosemary between your fingers before adding it to the pitcher to help release the oils.

ROSEMARY LEMONADE

~Serves 6 to 8

Zest and juice of 12 Eureka or Meyer lemons

1 cup superfine sugar

2 rosemary sprigs

Crushed ice

Pour the lemon juice into a large pitcher. Add the zest and sugar and stir until the sugar is fully dissolved.

Add the rosemary and ice and top up with cold water. Stir well and serve.

All you need to make limoncello is a bottle of vodka, half a dozen lemons, and some sugar. I make it every year when the Eurekas are at their best, but you can also make it with Meyer lemons for a more fragrant, sweeter liquor.

LIMONCELLO

~Makes about 4¹/₂ cups

6 Eureka lemons

1 (750 ml) bottle high-quality vodka

1 cup sugar

1¹/₂ cups water

Using a razor-sharp vegetable peeler, remove the peel from the lemons in long strips. Make sure you remove only the colored portion of the peel, with no bitter white pith attached. Cut the lemons in half and juice.

Pour the juice into a large, sterilized jar and add the peel. Pour in the vodka and stir to mix well. Cover the jar with plastic wrap and leave at room temperature for 2 weeks.

After the 2 weeks have passed, place the sugar in a saucepan, add the water, and bring to a boil over medium-high heat. Reduce the heat to a simmer and cook, stirring occasionally, for about 10 minutes, until the sugar has dissolved. Set the syrup aside to cool completely.

Pour the cooled sugar syrup into the vodka mixture and mix well. Let stand for 1 hour to infuse.

Line a fine-mesh sieve with cheesecloth, then strain the vodka mixture through the sieve and decant into 1 or more sterilized bottles with screw top lids. Label and store in a cool, dark cupboard for up to 1 year.

Lime | 31

Lime

Limes are small but they pack a big punch, adding a welcome burst of flavor to the simplest dish or drink. You would never think of biting into a spicy taco without a squeeze of lime, or of drinking a mojito without a tangle of muddled limes sitting on the bottom of the glass.

The lime that you most commonly see at your local store is the *Bearss*, also known as the Persian lime. It is juicy, fairly acidic, and has a smooth, thin peel, greenish yellow flesh, and no seeds.

The *Key lime*, also known as the West Indian lime, is smaller and more acidic than the Bearss and has seeds. It contributes its sharp flavor—both tart and sour with just a hint of sweetness—to a host of cocktails, a role that has earned it the nickname "bartender's lime."

The *makrut lime*, also known as the kaffir lime, is prized by cooks for its highly aromatic, tart, dark green leaves and its gloriously knobby, fragrant peel. Both the leaves and the peel are widely used to flavor dishes. Its juice has an overpowering flavor, however, so it is only rarely used in cooking. If you are bottling fresh fruits, such as plums or peaches, slip a couple of makrut lime leaves into each jar. They will deepen the flavor of the fruits. Look for fresh makrut limes and fresh or frozen leaves in stores specializing in Southeast Asian foods.

Finally, we have the quirky *finger lime*: shaped like its name, it has dark, thin skin, and flesh that pops like a citrus version of caviar when you eat it. Native to Australia, it is currently the darling of the restaurant world, both because of its resemblance to sturgeon roe and its amazing taste. If you should come across some finger limes, be careful when using them, however, as they can add a potent sourness.

Once you have a cache of these different types of limes on hand, try them in any one of the fragrant recipes on the following pages.

Start the day with a bowl full of sunshine and tropical flavors. Add spices, like cardamom, star anise, or cinnamon, and nuts, like almonds, macadamias, cashews, or hazelnuts, as well as other candied citrus, to make it your own.

TROPICAL GRANOLA WITH CANDIED LIME

~Makes 5 cups

6 tablespoons coconut oil, plus more for brushing

3 cups old-fashioned rolled oats

2 cups unsweetened dried coconut flakes

1/2 cup raw sunflower seeds

1/3 cup chia seeds

1/2 cup finely chopped dried mango

1/3 cup finely chopped candied lime (page 165)

3/4 cup honey

Preheat the oven to 300°F. Brush a large sheet pan with coconut oil.

In a large bowl, combine the oats, coconut flakes, sunflower seeds, and chia seeds and stir to mix well.

In a small saucepan, warm the honey and coconut oil over low heat. Pour over the granola and stir well to coat evenly.

Spread the granola in a single layer on the prepared sheet pan. Bake for 30 minutes, stirring halfway through. The granola should be lightly toasted.

Remove from the oven and add the mango and candied lime, stirring to combine. Let cool completely. Transfer to an airtight container and store at room temperature. It will keep for up to 3 weeks.

One of the easiest things to make is ricotta, and it can be used in so many delicious dishes—although it seems simplest is best. Here, it's perfumed with lime oil and served with crusty bread.

FARMHOUSE RICOTTA WITH PERSIAN LIME OIL

~Makes about 4 cups

4 quarts whole milk

2 cups heavy cream

1/3 cup freshly squeezed lemon juice

Sea salt and freshly ground black pepper

Persian lime oil (page 161), for drizzling

Crusty bread, for serving

In a large pot, combine the milk and cream, then clip a candy thermometer onto the side of the pot (or monitor with an instant-read thermometer). Place over medium heat and heat, stirring occasionally, to 190°F.

Remove from the heat, add the lemon juice, and slowly stir for a few turns. Cover the pot with a clean dish towel and set aside at room temperature for 1 hour. The liquid will have separated into milky white curds and watery ivory-colored whey.

Line a large sieve with cheesecloth and place over a bowl large enough to catch the whey. Gently pour the ricotta curds and whey into the sieve and let drain for 30 minutes. For a denser cheese, let drain for 2 hours or for up to overnight in the refrigerator. (The longer you drain the cheese, the smaller the yield.)

Spoon the ricotta into a serving bowl, season with salt and pepper, and drizzle generously with the lime oil. Serve with crusty bread.

To store the ricotta, transfer to a glass container with a tight-fitting lid and refrigerate for up to 6 days. Save the whey and use in bread or other baking recipes; store it in an airtight container and refrigerate for up to 4 days or freeze for up to 3 months.

Ceviche is the national dish of Peru—first introduced by the Moorish women who cooked for the conquistadors—and even has a day named after it. Freshly caught seafood is marinated in citrusy mixtures. Halibut is a good firm white fish for this dish, but you can use any kind of seafood you like. Just make sure it is the freshest sushi grade.

HALIBUT CEVICHE WITH LIME & TEQUILA

~Serves 2 to 4

1 pound fresh sushi-grade halibut fillet

Zest and juice of 4 limes

2 tablespoons tequila

2 radishes, thinly sliced

Edible flowers, for garnish

¼ cup extra virgin olive oil

Pink salt, for sprinkling

Rinse the fish and pat dry with paper towels. Place on a cutting board and using a razor-sharp knife, cut the fish against the grain into paper-thin slices.

Arrange the fish slices in a ceramic dish. In a small bowl, whisk together the lime zest and juice and tequila and pour over the fish. Cover and refrigerate for 3 hours.

Remove the fish from the fridge. To serve, using a fork, remove the fish from the marinade and arrange on a serving platter. Top with the radishes and flowers. Drizzle with the olive oil and finish with a sprinkle of pink salt.

Halloumi is a wonderful salty cheese from Cyprus that is great to cook with because it holds its shape when heated. Add a splash of ouzo to deepen the flavors of this dish. Top with the fragrant salsa and serve with icy-cold beer.

HALLOUMI WITH PRESERVED LIME, CUCUMBER & MINT SALSA

~Serves 4

SALSA

2 preserved lime quarters (page 54)

1 Persian cucumber, diced

1 cup loosely packed fresh mint leaves, torn

¼ cup extra virgin olive oil

Juice of 1 lime

2 tablespoons olive oil

1 pound halloumi cheese, sliced into ¼-inch-thick pieces

¼ cup ouzo

Ground sumac, for sprinkling

Toasted pita bread

To make the salsa, rinse the lime quarters under cool running water, remove and discard the flesh, and finely dice the skins. In a bowl, combine the lime skins, cucumber, mint, oil, and lime juice and mix well. Set aside.

Place a large cast-iron or other heavy frying pan over high heat until smoking. Turn down the heat to medium, pour in the oil, swirl the pan to coat the bottom evenly, and then carefully add the cheese slices in a single layer. Halloumi cooks quickly, so check it almost immediately. When the underside is golden brown, flip the slices and cook on the second side for 1 to 2 minutes, until golden brown. Pour the ouzo into the pan, swirl, and allow the alcohol to burn off and reduce, about 2 minutes.

Place the cheese on a serving platter and top with the salsa. Sprinkle with the sumac and serve immediately with the pita.

In this spin on the famous Neapolitan dish *spaghetti alle vongole*, the addition of lime juice and zest delivers a citrusy spark and calms the heat of the jalapeño chile. Scrub the clams well before cooking and discard any that don't close to the touch.

LINGUINE WITH CLAMS & LIME

~Serves 4

Sea salt and freshly ground black pepper

1 pound dried linguine

2 tablespoons olive oil

2 cloves garlic, minced

1 small yellow onion, finely diced

1 jalapeño chile, finely chopped

1½ cups dry white wine

Zest and juice of 3 limes

2 pounds Manila or other small clams, scrubbed

1 cup coarsely chopped fresh flat-leaf parsley leaves

Bring a large pot of water to a boil and add 1 teaspoon of salt. Add the linguine and cook for about 9 minutes, until al dente.

While the pasta is cooking, in a large sauté pan, heat the oil over medium heat. Add the garlic, onion, and chile and sauté for a few minutes, until the onion is translucent. Pour in the wine and bring to a boil. Add the lime zest and juice and stir well. Add the clams, cover with a tight-fitting lid, and cook for 3 to 5 minutes, until the clams open. Uncover and discard any clams that did not open. Turn off the heat.

Drain the pasta and add to the clams. Cover the pan and rest for 5 minutes, so the pasta soaks up the juices.

Season with salt and pepper and spoon into individual bowls. Sprinkle with the parsley and serve.

Hypnotic spices laced with lime and creamy coconut make this curry a one-pot wonder. This dish conjures up vivid memories of a similar curry I ate in a beach shack on the island of Guadeloupe in the Caribbean many years ago. So good that I went back the next day for more.

LIME CHICKEN CURRY

~Serves 4

4 tablespoons coconut oil, melted

Zest and juice of
2 large limes

2 tablespoons curry powder

2 teaspoons chile powder

Pinch of sea salt

6 skin-on, bone-in chicken thighs

1 yellow onion, coarsely chopped

1 (14-ounce) can coconut milk

½ cup unsweetened dried coconut flakes

1 cup cilantro leaves

In a large glass or ceramic bowl, whisk together 2 tablespoons of the coconut oil, the lime zest and juice, curry powder, chile powder, and salt. Add the chicken thighs and turn to coat them evenly with the mixture. Cover and refrigerate for at least 4 hours or for up to 24 hours.

Remove the chicken from the refrigerator and bring to room temperature.

Heat a Dutch oven over medium-high and add the remaining 2 tablespoons of coconut oil. When the oil is smoking, add the chicken, skin side down, and turn down the heat to medium. Brown the chicken for 5 minutes, then turn over. Add the onion and continue to brown the chicken for another 5 minutes.

Pour in the coconut milk and stir in the coconut flakes. Reduce the heat to a simmer and cook for 15 minutes, until the chicken is cooked through. Remove the pan from the heat, cover it with the lid, and allow it to rest for 5 minutes. Remove the lid, sprinkle with the cilantro leaves, and serve.

Wintertime is crab season, which coincides nicely with much of citrus season. Enjoy cracking the shells and dipping the sweet crabmeat into a spicy sauce. Serve this dish with plenty of cold beer!

DUNGENESS CRAB WITH LIME & CHILE DIPPING SAUCE

~Serves 2

DIPPING SAUCE

2 tablespoons rice vinegar

3 tablespoons freshly squeezed lime juice

2 tablespoons soy sauce

2 tablespoons peeled and grated fresh ginger

1 tablespoon sugar

1 red serrano chile, finely chopped

¼ cup white wine vinegar

2 live Dungeness crabs, about 3 pounds each

2 limes, cut into wedges

To make the dipping sauce, in a small bowl, combine the vinegar, lime juice, soy sauce, ginger, sugar, and chile. Whisk together until the sugar dissolves. Set aside.

Bring a large pot of water to a boil over high heat and add the vinegar. One at a time, place the crabs in the pot so they are completely submerged. Cook the crabs for 20 minutes; their shells will turn bright red-orange when they are done. Remove them from the pot using tongs. Allow to sit for a few minutes to cool so they are easier to handle.

To clean the crab, turn it belly side up on a cutting board and remove the triangular piece of shell (the "apron"). Then, remove the top shell in one piece. Remove and discard the gills and the mouthpiece. Peel away any loose fragments, then rinse off the body to remove any foam or entrails.

Serve each crab on a plate along with the dipping sauce, lime wedges, and a nutcracker for cracking the shells.

Soaked in zesty lime syrup, this nutty, perfumed cake begs to be eaten along with a good cup of strong Turkish coffee. It is satisfying on its own or served with a dollop of Greek yogurt and fresh fruit.

TURKISH YOGURT CAKE WITH LIME SYRUP & PISTACHIOS

~Serves 6 to 8

2 cups self-rising flour

1 teaspoon baking powder

$1/2$ cup plus 3 tablespoons unsalted butter, at room temperature

1 cup sugar

3 eggs, at room temperature

1 cup plain Greek yogurt

$1/4$ cup pistachios, finely ground

LIME SYRUP

1 cup sugar

1 cup water

1 lime, thinly sliced

Preheat the oven to 350°F. Line the bottom and sides of a 10 by 5-inch loaf pan with parchment paper, then grease the paper with unsalted butter.

In a bowl, sift together the flour and baking powder and set aside. In the bowl of a stand mixer fitted with the paddle attachment, cream together the butter and sugar on medium speed, until light and fluffy. Add the eggs, one at a time, and beat until smooth. Add the yogurt and continue to beat until well combined. Reduce the speed to low and slowly add the flour mixture, beating until well combined. Stir in the pistachios and pour the batter into the prepared loaf pan.

Bake the cake for about 1 hour, until a thin wooden skewer inserted into the center comes out clean.

To make the lime syrup, in a small saucepan, combine the sugar and water over medium-high heat and bring to a boil, stirring to dissolve the sugar. Continue to boil for 5 minutes, then reduce the heat to medium-low. Add the lime slices and gently simmer for about 20 minutes, until they are translucent. Remove from the heat and let stand.

continued

TURKISH YOGURT CAKE WITH
LIME SYRUP & PISTACHIOS
continued

Remove the cake from the oven and place on a wire rack. Using the skewer, pierce the top all over and let cool for 20 minutes.

Remove the limes from the syrup, transfer them to a small bowl, cover, and let stand at room temperature until ready to use. Drizzle the syrup over the cake. Loosely cover with plastic wrap and leave overnight.

The next day, invert the pan onto a serving plate, lift off the pan, and peel off the parchment. Turn the cake right side up and arrange the reserved lime slices on top. Slice thickly to serve.

This crowd-pleaser is a nice twist on traditional rice pudding, with creamy coconut milk taking the place of cow's milk and makrut zest, juice, and leaves adding an exotic aroma and flavor.

COCONUT RICE PUDDING WITH MAKRUT LIMES

~Serves 4

½ cup jasmine rice

2½ cups coconut milk

2 tablespoons superfine sugar

Zest and juice of 1 makrut lime

4 makrut lime leaves

⅓ cup unsweetened dried coconut flakes, toasted

In a saucepan, combine the rice, coconut milk, sugar, and lime zest and juice and bring to a boil over medium-high heat, stirring until the sugar dissolves. Reduce the heat to low, add the lime leaves, and simmer gently for 15 minutes.

Remove the pan from the heat and remove and discard the lime leaves. Let the pudding stand for 5 minutes, then spoon into individual bowls. Top with the coconut flakes and serve warm.

The next time you see Key limes at your local market, scoop them up and make this classic pie. Add a dash of the Caribbean with toasted coconut and lime zest.

KEY LIME PIE

~Serves 6

CRUST

12 graham crackers

2 tablespoons light brown sugar

$1/2$ cup unsalted butter, melted

FILLING AND TOPPING

4 egg yolks

1 (14-ounce) can sweetened condensed milk

$1/2$ cup freshly squeezed Key lime juice

$1/2$ cup heavy cream

$1/2$ cup unsweetened dried coconut flakes, toasted

Grated lime zest, for garnish

Preheat the oven to 350°F.

To make the crust, in a food processor, combine the graham crackers and sugar and process until the crackers are reduced to crumbs. Add the melted butter and pulse until well combined.

Pour the crumb mixture into a 9-inch pie pan and press it evenly over the bottom and sides of the pan. Bake for 10 minutes, until golden. Transfer to a wire rack to cool.

To make the filling, in a bowl, whisk together the egg yolks and condensed milk until blended. Pour in the lime juice and whisk until well combined and smooth. Pour into the cooled pie crust.

Bake the pie for about 15 minutes, until the filling is set. Transfer to a wire rack and let cool completely. Cover and refrigerate for at least 6 hours or for up to 24 hours.

To make the topping, just before serving, pour the cream into a bowl. Using a handheld mixer, beat the cream until stiff peaks form.

Pile the cream on top of the cold pie, sprinkle with the coconut flakes, and garnish with the lime zest. Cut into wedges to serve.

Crunchy and spicy-sweet, these irresistible nuts are ideal for nibbling alongside cocktails and are also delicious sprinkled over leafy green salads or enjoyed as a snack on their own.

LIME & CHILE SALTED ALMONDS

~Makes 2 cups

2 cups unsalted organic almonds

Zest of 3 limes

1 tablespoon chile powder

1/2 cup firmly packed light brown sugar

1/4 cup maple syrup

1 1/2 tablespoons coarse sea salt

Preheat the oven to 375°F.

In a bowl, combine the almonds, lime zest, chile powder, sugar, and maple syrup and stir until the nuts are evenly coated with the other ingredients. Spread out the nut mixture on a sheet pan.

Roast the nuts for about 8 minutes, until they are brown and the sugar is bubbling.

Remove the almonds from the oven, sprinkle with the salt, and stir with a wooden spoon. Let cool completely before serving. The nuts will keep in an airtight container at room temperature for up to 1 week.

It's easy to put up a jar of these flavorful limes, and the floral fragrance of their skins will brighten up any dish. If you like, add a few black peppercorns and citrus leaves to the jar, but not so many that the lime flavor will be overpowered. This same method can also be used to preserve lemons.

PRESERVED LIMES

~Makes 1 quart

1 cup sea salt

6 limes, quartered lengthwise

Juice of 6 limes

Pour about 2 tablespoons of the salt onto the bottom of a sterilized 1-quart jar with a tight-fitting lid and top with a layer of lime wedges. Continue to fill the jar with alternating layers of salt and lime wedges, packing the fruit down as you go and finishing with a layer of salt. Pour the lime juice into the jar. If the limes are not covered by the juice, add water as needed to cover them.

Screw on the lid tightly and store the limes in the refrigerator for 1 month before using. They will keep for up to 6 months longer. To use the limes, rinse off the salt under cool running water, remove and discard the flesh, and use the skins as desired.

Lassi, which originates from India, is a delicious, nutritious thirst quencher for a hot day. Here, I've used coconut milk instead of the traditional yogurt for a nice twist on such a delicious drink. Sometimes spices like turmeric, cardamom, or cumin are added, all of which are believed to have important medicinal properties.

LIME & COCONUT LASSI

~Serves 2

1 ripe, juicy lime, coarsely chopped

1 (14-ounce) can coconut milk

2 tablespoons honey

4 mint sprigs

TO SERVE
Crushed ice

In a blender, combine the lime, coconut milk, honey, and mint and blend until smooth. Pour into 2 tall glasses filled with crushed ice, and serve.

When the hot summer sun starts to fade, it's time for cocktails. And there is no better way to end the day than with a mojito: tall chilled glasses filled with ice, muddled limes, mint leaves, and rum. Sit back and watch the sunset.

HAVANA MOJITO

~Serves 2

2 limes, quartered

4 teaspoons cane sugar

½ cup loosely packed fresh mint leaves

Crushed ice, for serving

4 ounces white rum

Club soda, for topping up

Divide the lime quarters and sugar evenly between 2 tall glasses. Muddle the mixture with a muddler or the back of a wooden spoon to release all of the citrus juice and oils.

Rub the mint leaves between your fingers to bruise them and release their oils. Divide the mint between the glasses and stir to mix.

Fill the glasses with the crushed ice and then divide the rum between the glasses. Top off each glass with club soda, stir, and serve. Salud!

Orange | 59

Orange

A new crop of oranges starts to show up at farmers' markets in late fall, and by the time the holiday season arrives, the stalls are creaking with the weight of freshly picked ripe and juicy fruits. These jeweled delights are Mother Nature's way of brightening up the long, dark winter months with sweet delightful citrus that can turn any dish around.

We have chosen the most popular and easy-to-find orange varieties for the recipes in this chapter. If you come across others, however, feel free to substitute them. You can also use orange leaves in the kitchen, as we do in the wine on page 93. And even orange flowers can be put to work, as Victoria's friend Fardeneh does. She spreads sheets out under her orange trees to catch the blossoms, which then end up in a sweet sugar syrup as a jam. The gentle and romantic way in which the flowers are collected adds to the beauty of the preserves.

More than half of all the oranges grown in the United States are *Valencias*. They have sweet, juicy pulp, brightly colored juice, and thin skins, making them ideal for juicing and eating out of hand. Valencias are picked from spring into fall, with the peak of the harvest in the summer months. We use Valencias for everything from bread pudding (page 83) and marmalade (page 71) to cake (page 75).

Navel oranges have thicker skins than Valencias, making them easier to peel. They are also sweet, have meaty, bright orange flesh, and usually contain no or very few seeds, making them an excellent eating orange. The fragrant juice of the navel is especially delicious in sorbets and granitas, and the peel is excellent candied (page 165). The *Cara Cara orange*, a type of

navel, has all of the qualities of its kin, plus beautiful pinkish red flesh and a pleasant berry-like tang, making it a wonderful choice for salads.

Like the Cara Cara, *blood oranges* boast colorful flesh, which can range from a mottled orange and pink to the ruby red of the Moro type. The peel is colorful as well, varying from a hint of rose to a deep red blush. Blood oranges typically explode with a sweet, slightly tart taste reminiscent of freshly picked berries. We like to use them in salads and desserts and in our icy-cold margaritas (page 90).

The two best-known sour, or bitter, oranges are the *Seville* and the *bergamot*. Both of them have thick, bumpy skins, relatively dry flesh, and an extremely tart flavor, and neither one of them belongs in a fruit bowl. Sevilles are most commonly used to make tangy marmalade laced with sliced peel. They can also be cooked in a thick sugar syrup for spooning over ice cream or swirling through yogurt, or fashioned into sauces, candies, and liqueurs.

Of all of the oranges described here, the bergamot will be the most difficult to find. It is cultivated almost exclusively in southern Italy, though a handful of California citrus growers have planted some trees in recent years. Bergamot is primarily known for the intensely aromatic essential oils extracted from its skin and used for flavoring Earl Grey tea. But the peel can also be used for making marmalade, preserved in salt or sugar, or added to tea or a tisane, and the juice can be used in modest amounts in vinaigrettes, sauces, syrups, and marinades.

This is one of those beautiful, timeless salads. The vibrant colors and sweetness of the oranges contrast perfectly with the salty ricotta. Change up the greens with more earthy flavors, such as watercress and baby kale.

CARA CARA & BLOOD ORANGE SALAD WITH RICOTTA SALATA

~Serves 4

3 Cara Cara oranges

3 blood oranges

4 cups mixed salad greens (such as arugula and mizuna)

6 ounces ricotta salata cheese, crumbled

Juice of 1 blood orange

¼ cup extra virgin olive oil

Freshly cracked black pepper

To peel the oranges, using a sharp knife, cut a thin slice off both ends of the fruit to reveal the flesh and stand the fruit upright. Then, following the curve of the fruit, cut downward to remove the peel and white pith, rotating the fruit as you work until all of the peel and pith is cut away.

Reserve the peels for another use, such as Candied Peel (page 165). Thinly slice the oranges crosswise.

Arrange the orange slices in a shallow serving bowl. Top with the salad greens and sprinkle with the ricotta salata.

In a small bowl, whisk together the blood orange juice and oil until blended, then drizzle over the salad. Sprinkle with pepper, toss gently, and serve immediately.

Here, a taste of Spain—oranges from its sunny south—and a taste of Italy—polenta from its northern cornfields—join forces with a catch of fresh sardines. It's delicious with a cold white Rioja.

GRILLED SARDINES WITH ORANGE & POLENTA

~Serves 4

12 fresh sardines

2 navel oranges

½ cup coarsely chopped flat-leaf parsley

2 cloves garlic, minced

¼ cup plus 2 tablespoons extra virgin olive oil

1 cup fine-grind polenta or cornmeal

Working with 1 sardine at a time, place it on a cutting board. Using a sharp knife, cut the sardine open along the belly, working from head to tail, to create a cavity for the filling. Remove the entrails and rinse under cold water. Pat dry. Repeat with the remaining sardines.

Zest the oranges and set the zest aside. Then, peel the oranges, making sure no white pith remains. Coarsely chop the flesh of the oranges and transfer to a bowl. Add the parsley, the garlic, and the ¼ cup of olive oil and stir to combine.

Spread the polenta in a shallow bowl. Stuff each sardine with about 1 tablespoon of the orange mixture and gently press it closed. Roll the sardines in the polenta to coat loosely, then drizzle with the remaining 2 tablespoons of oil.

Heat a large stove-top grill pan over high heat until smoking (if you do not have a large pan, use 2 pans or cook in batches). Lay the sardines in the pan, turn down the heat to medium, and cook for 5 minutes. Carefully flip the sardines over and cook for 5 minutes longer, until the skins are crispy and brown.

Transfer the sardines to a platter and serve immediately, with the remaining orange mixture alongside.

I like to dish up this robust stew when winter comes around and it's time for leisurely, slow-cooked dinners—preferably alongside an earthy red wine. A generous sprinkle of orange gremolata brightens the depths of the sauce.

OSSO BUCO WITH ORANGE GREMOLATA

~Serves 4 to 6

All-purpose flour, for dusting

Sea salt and freshly cracked black pepper

6 pieces veal shank, each 2 inches thick

¼ cup olive oil

2 cloves garlic, minced

1 yellow onion, diced

4 thyme sprigs

2 bay leaves

3 cups veal or chicken stock

2 cups dry white wine

1 cup pitted green olives

GREMOLATA

Zest of 1 navel orange

½ cup firmly packed flat-leaf parsley leaves, torn

3 cloves garlic, minced

Preheat the oven to 350°F.

Season the flour with salt and pepper. Dredge the shanks in the flour, shaking off the excess.

In a large Dutch oven, heat the oil over medium-high heat. When the oil is hot, add the shanks and cook, turning once, for about 5 minutes total, until browned on both sides. Transfer to a plate.

Add the garlic and onion and cook, stirring often, for about 5 minutes, until golden brown. Return the shanks to the pot, add the thyme, bay leaves, stock, and wine, and bring to a boil. Remove from the heat and add the olives. Cover and place in the preheated oven and cook for 1½ hours, until the meat is fork-tender.

To make the gremolata, place the orange zest, parsley, and garlic in a small bowl and mix well. Cover and place in the refrigerator until ready to use.

Remove the pot from the oven and let the osso buco rest for 10 minutes. Spoon into individual bowls, sprinkle with the gremolata, and serve immediately.

Valencia oranges and Campari are a heavenly match, pairing the sweetness of the fruit with the bitterness of the aperitif. But you can successfully match other spirits with oranges as well, such as Cointreau, bourbon, or tequila.

ORANGE & CAMPARI MARMALADE

~Makes about 4 half pints

2¹/₂ pounds Valencia oranges (about 8 small oranges)

Zest and juice of 1 lemon

6 cups water

2 pounds superfine sugar

¹/₄ cup Campari

Place a small plate in the freezer.

Halve each orange from top to bottom, then cut each half lengthwise into 4 wedges. Thinly slice each wedge crosswise, discarding any seeds.

Put the oranges, lemon zest and juice, and water in a preserving pan or other large, nonreactive pan and bring to a boil over high heat. Turn down the heat to medium and simmer uncovered, stirring occasionally, for 2 hours.

Add the sugar and Campari, raise the heat to high, and bring to a boil, stirring continuously until the sugar has dissolved completely. Boil for 10 minutes.

At this point, the bubbles should be small and the mixture should be dense and beginning to darken. Take the chilled plate from the freezer, drop a small spoonful of the marmalade onto it, and return it to the freezer for 2 minutes. Return it to the freezer and let it set for 2 minutes. The dollop should be thick and syrupy. If it is still liquidy, boil the marmalade for another 5 minutes and test again. Repeat until you have the desired consistency.

continued

ORANGE & CAMPARI MARMALADE
continued

Stir the marmalade occasionally to prevent sticking to the pan. (Alternatively you can test the marmalade with a candy thermometer, which should register 220°F when ready.)

Remove the pan from the heat and let the marmalade rest for 10 minutes. This helps to ensure that the orange slices are suspended evenly throughout the marmalade. Using a large spoon, skim off any scum from the surface, as it can make the marmalade cloudy.

Preheat the oven to 250°F.

Pour the marmalade into warm sterilized jars leaving ½-inch of space. Screw the lids on. Wipe the jars clean and place them in a baking dish. Place in the preheated oven for 25 minutes to seal.

Remove the jars from the oven and set on a cooling rack. Leave undisturbed until they have cooled completely. You will hear a ping sound as each lid seals. Check to make sure that the center of the lid is concave. Store the jars in a cool, dark cupboard for up to 1 year. If a seal is not good, store the jar in the refrigerator and use within 3 weeks.

Earl Grey tea is infused with bergamot oil, which gives it its wonderful perfume and unique taste. Here, pears are poached in the tea and take on the heady aroma of the bergamot. They're exquisite served with a spoonful or two of cream.

EARL GREY POACHED PEARS

~Serves 6

4 cups water

3 Earl Grey tea bags

4 firm but ripe pears
(such as Bosc or Anjou)

2 cups sugar

In a Dutch oven, bring the water to a boil over high heat. Add the tea bags, cover, and turn off the heat. Allow the tea to infuse for 20 minutes.

Meanwhile, peel the pears and quarter them lengthwise. With a sharp paring knife, core, remove the seeds, and set the pears aside.

Remove the tea bags, squeezing out any excess liquid, and discard the bags. Return the pan to medium-high heat and add the sugar. Bring to a boil, then reduce the heat to medium and simmer, stirring until the sugar has completely dissolved.

Add the pears to the simmering liquid, cover, and simmer for 6 to 8 minutes, until tender. Using a slotted spoon, transfer the pears to a bowl. Return the liquid to a boil over medium-high heat and cook for 10 to 15 minutes, until reduced by half to a thick syrup.

Remove from the heat, and pour the syrup over the pears. Let cool to room temperature before serving. The pears can be refrigerated for up to 1 week.

There's a farm stand near Victoria's house that sells all kinds of oranges, and it's the inspiration for this cake, which uses a variety of oranges to give it a colorful, jeweled top. Soaked in syrup and with the herbal taste of rosemary, it is delicious served with tea as an afternoon treat.

ORANGE & ROSEMARY POLENTA CAKE

~Serves 6 to 8

1¼ cups sugar

¼ cup water

2 Valencia oranges, thinly sliced

2 blood oranges, thinly sliced

2 cups all-purpose flour

½ cup fine-grind polenta

1½ teaspoons baking powder

2 tablespoons finely chopped fresh rosemary

1 cup unsalted butter, at room temperature

4 eggs

Preheat the oven to 350°F. Butter a 10-inch springform pan. In a saucepan, combine ½ cup of the sugar and the water and heat over medium-high heat. Allow the sugar to dissolve without stirring. Boil the mixture for about 5 minutes, until it starts turning golden brown. Remove from the heat, pour the syrup into the prepared pan, and swirl the cake pan to cover the bottom.

Arrange the orange slices in concentric circles on the syrup, overlapping them and covering the bottom of the pan completely.

In a bowl, stir together the flour, polenta, baking powder, and rosemary and set aside. In another bowl, using a handheld mixer, beat together the butter and the remaining ¾ cup of sugar on low speed until creamy, then increase the speed to high and beat until the mixture is light, fluffy, and pale ivory. On medium speed, add the eggs one at a time, beating well after each addition, until combined.

Reduce the speed to low and add the polenta and flour mixture a little at a time, scraping down the sides of the bowl, until combined.

Spoon the mixture over the orange slices and bake for 40 to 45 minutes, until a wooden skewer comes out clean. Remove from the oven and allow to cool for 15 minutes. Invert the cake onto a serving platter and serve warm.

One bite of these heavenly scented delights and you are immediately transported to an orange grove in full bloom. The orange blossom meringue disappears on your tongue and you are left with the lingering taste of rich dark chocolate. Indulgent? Yes, but so easy to make.

ORANGE BLOSSOM MACARONS

~Makes about 28 macarons

1 cup almond meal or finely ground blanched almonds

1½ cups confectioners' sugar

3 egg whites (about ⅓ cup)

Pinch of cream of tartar

¼ cup granulated sugar

2 drops orange food coloring

3 drops orange blossom water

GANACHE

1 cup heavy cream

8 ounces good quality dark chocolate (preferably 70% cocoa), finely chopped

1 tablespoon unsalted butter

3 drops orange blossom water

Line 2 sheet pans with parchment paper. Fit two pastry bags with ½-inch round tips.

In a food processor, combine the almond meal and confectioners' sugar and process until fine and blended. Sift the mixture into a bowl, pushing any lumps through the screen with a rubber spatula. Set aside.

In the bowl of a stand mixer fitted with the whisk attachment, beat the egg whites on high speed until frothy. Add the cream of tartar and continue to beat until you have stiff peaks. Reduce the speed to medium and slowly add the granulated sugar. Continue to beat until thick, glossy peaks form. Add the food coloring and the orange blossom water and continue to mix until the color is uniform. Using a spatula, fold the almond meal mixture into the egg white mixture until completely combined.

Spoon the mixture into one of the prepared pastry bags and pipe 1-inch circles onto the the prepared sheet pans, spacing them 1 inch apart. Slam the sheet pans on the counter to remove air bubbles. Set aside to harden for 20 minutes.

continued

ORANGE BLOSSOM MACARONS
continued

Preheat the oven to 350°F. Bake the macarons for 10 minutes, until firm to the touch. Let cool completely on the pans.

To make the ganache, in a small saucepan, bring the cream to a simmer over medium heat. Add the chocolate, remove the pan from the heat, and stir until the chocolate has melted. Add the butter and orange blossom water and continue to stir until the sauce is glossy. Pour into a bowl and refrigerate until the ganache has thickened slightly but is still pliable. Spoon the ganache into the second prepared pastry bag.

Take one macaron half and pipe a thin layer of ganache onto it, then top with another macaron. Continue until all the macarons are filled. They can be served now or stored for up to a week in an airtight container in the refrigerator.

Eat this enticingly rich dessert slowly to savor each spoonful. A little pot of this perfumed cream needs only a spoon to enjoy. In place of candied bergamot, you can top with other candied citrus, such as candied lime, tangerine, or lemon.

BERGAMOT PANNA COTTA

~Serves 4 to 6

1 cup whole milk

4 Earl Grey tea bags

3 tablespoons warm water

2½ teaspoons powdered gelatin

2 cups heavy cream

¾ cup sugar

Candied bergamot peel (page 165), for garnish

In a small saucepan, bring the milk to a boil over medium heat. Add the tea bags, immediately remove from the heat, and let steep for 1 hour. Remove the tea bags, squeezing them gently to release all of the liquid into the pan, and discard the bags.

Put the water in a small bowl, sprinkle the gelatin over the top, and let stand for 1 to 2 minutes to soften.

Return the pan to medium heat and add the cream and sugar. Bring the mixture to a boil, then reduce the heat to medium, stirring continuously until the sugar has completely dissolved, about 5 minutes. Whisk in the gelatin until dissolved, then remove from the heat.

Pour the mixture into 4 to 6 ramekins or small bowls and let cool to room temperature. Cover and refrigerate for 4 hours, until set. Serve topped with candied peel.

Enjoy these caramelized orange slices as a dessert with lashings of crème fraîche or a scoop of homemade vanilla ice cream. They also pair well with roasted pork or duck.

HONEY ORANGES WITH LAVENDER FLOWERS

~Serves 4 to 6

6 oranges

1/2 cup orange blossom honey

2 tablespoons olive oil

2 drops orange blossom water (optional)

1/4 cup fresh lavender flowers

Preheat the oven to 400°F. Zest the oranges and set the zest aside. Then peel the oranges, being careful to remove all of the white pith with the remains of the peel. Cut the oranges crosswise into 1-inch-thick slices.

Layer the orange slices in a baking dish. In a small bowl, whisk together the honey, oil, and 1/4 cup of the zest, reserving any remaining zest for another use. Whisk in the orange blossom water. Pour the honey mixture evenly over the oranges.

Roast the oranges for 45 minutes, until caramelized. Remove from the oven, sprinkle with the lavender, and serve.

Put together this brightly flavored dessert when the weather turns chilly and comfort food is a must. The marmalade plays off the creaminess of the custard and then finishes with a slight crunch from the toasted bread. If you don't have time to make the marmalade, use a high-quality store-bought brand.

VALENCIA ORANGE BREAD & BUTTER PUDDING

~Serves 6

4 tablespoons unsalted butter, at room temperature

12 slices white country-style bread

½ cup Orange & Campari Marmalade (page 71)

5 eggs

1 vanilla bean, halved lengthwise

1 cup whole milk

1 cup heavy cream

¼ cup firmly packed dark brown sugar, plus more for sprinkling

Crème fraîche, for serving

Butter a shallow baking dish. Butter both sides of each bread slice, using all the butter. Spread the marmalade on one side of 6 of the slices of bread. Take the other 6 slices of bread and place them, butter side up, on top of the marmalade slices to make 6 sandwiches. Cut each sandwich diagonally in half and arrange the sandwich halves in the prepared dish.

Crack the eggs into a bowl. Using the tip of a knife, scrape the vanilla seeds from the bean halves into the bowl, and whisk the eggs until blended. Add the milk, cream, and sugar and whisk until well combined. Pour the mixture evenly over the bread and sprinkle lightly with more sugar.

Cover and let stand at room temperature for 1 hour, until the bread soaks up the custard. Preheat the oven to 350°F.

Uncover the pudding and bake for about 50 minutes, until the custard has set. Remove from the oven and let cool slightly.

Serve warm, spooned into individual bowls. Top each serving with a dollop of crème fraîche.

This light and refreshing drink tastes great and is good for you. It can be dressed up in many ways, with fruits and spices, poured over homemade granola (page 35), or just drunk simply on its own.

ORANGE BLOSSOM ALMOND MILK

~Makes a scant 2 cups

1 cup unsalted organic almonds

2 cups water

1 tablespoon orange blossom honey

2 drops orange blossom water, or to taste

Put the almonds in a glass or ceramic bowl, pour in cold water to cover completely, and let soak for at least overnight or for up to 2 days.

Drain the nuts and transfer to a blender. Add the water and blend until smooth. Strain the mixture through a nut bag or a sieve lined with cheesecloth, squeezing out as much milk as possible from the almond meal. (You can spread the leftover almond meal on a sheet pan and dry it in a 200°F oven for about 25 minutes, then use it in baking cookies or homemade granola.)

Return the strained almond milk to the blender, add the honey and orange blossom water, and blend until well mixed. Use immediately, or store in an airtight container in the refrigerator for up to 4 days.

Bitters are a mainstay of the cocktail pantry, and they are sold in many flavors and colors. It's easy to make them at home by infusing citrus peels, along with herbs and spices, in vodka. Use thick-skinned oranges, such as navel, for the best result. Although bay is used here, thyme or rosemary would work as well.

ORANGE BITTERS

~Makes about 4 1/2 cups

4 large, thick-skinned oranges
2 fresh bay leaves
1 (750 ml) bottle vodka

SYRUP
2 cups sugar
1 cup water

TO SERVE
Ice
Citrus Salt (page 158)
Mint sprigs

Using a razor-sharp vegetable peeler, remove the zest from the oranges, leaving behind the white pith. Reserve the oranges for another use.

In a large, sterilized jar with a tight-fitting lid, combine the orange zest and bay leaves. Pour in the vodka, cover tightly, and store at room temperature for 3 weeks.

After the 3 weeks have passed, make the syrup. In a saucepan, combine the sugar and water and bring to a boil over medium-high heat, stirring to dissolve the sugar. Turn down the heat to medium-low and simmer, stirring occasionally, for 10 to 15 minutes, until the sugar has dissolved completely. Remove from the heat and let cool completely.

Using either a coffee filter or a fine-mesh sieve fitted with cheesecloth, strain the vodka mixture into a pitcher, discarding the solids. Add the cooled syrup, and stir to mix.

Decant the bitters into sterilized bottles, cap tightly, and store in a cool, dark place for 3 months before using. The bitters will keep for up to 1 year.

We like to serve this poured over ice in a citrus salt–rimmed glass, garnished with a sprig of mint.

A tisane is a botanical infusion, a deliciously refreshing drink. This rendition, with bergamot and mint, is a great pick-me-up on a hot afternoon. You can add sugar or honey for sweetness. If you can't find bergamot, strips of orange peel can be used.

BERGAMOT & MINT TISANE

~Serves 2

1 large bunch mint

Peel of ½ bergamot, removed in strips

Boiling water

TO SERVE
Sugar or honey (optional)

Put the mint and bergamot peel in a teapot, and cover with boiling water. Let steep for 5 minutes. Strain into cups, and serve with sugar or honey to sweeten, if desired.

What could be better than an icy-cold margarita, especially if it's made with vividly colored blood oranges? The fruit of the Moro is a divine deep red—almost burgundy—and looks spectacular in a chilled glass rimmed with pretty pink citrus salt.

ICY BLOOD ORANGE MARGARITA

~Serves 2

2 Moro blood oranges

1 tablespoon pink salt

1/2 cup tequila

1/4 cup Cointreau

3 cups crushed ice

Zest the oranges. On a small, flat saucer, mix together the zest and pink salt and set aside.

Peel the oranges, being careful to remove all of the white pith with the peel. Reserve a piece of the peel. Pull apart the oranges into quarters.

Have ready 2 chilled glasses. Run the reserved piece of peel around the rims of the glasses, and dip the rims into the citrus salt.

In a blender, combine the oranges, tequila, Cointreau, and ice and blend until smooth. Pour into the salted glasses and serve immediately.

Victoria made this beautiful *vin d'orange* for her wedding—
a very fitting drink for a very romantic, memorable
celebration among the orange groves of Ojai.

ORANGE WEDDING WINE

~Makes about 5 quarts

10 Valencia oranges

5 Eureka lemons

6 (750 ml) bottles rosé

1½ cups high-quality
brandy

1 vanilla bean, halved
lengthwise

1 handful of orange leaves

ORANGE SYRUP

4 Valencia oranges

3 cups sugar

3 cups water

TO SERVE

Ice

Orange twists, for garnish

Quarter the oranges and lemons lengthwise and place in a large
glass jar (at least 6-quart capacity) with a tight-fitting lid. Add the
rosé, brandy, vanilla bean, and orange leaves and stir well. Cap
the jar and store it in a dark, cool, dry place for 1 month.

Strain the liquid through a fine-mesh sieve, then decant into
sterilized bottles, cap tightly, and refrigerate. The wine will keep
for 1 year.

To make the orange syrup, using a razor-sharp vegetable peeler,
remove the zest from the oranges in long strips, leaving behind
any white pith.

In a saucepan, combine the orange zest, sugar, and water. Bring
to a boil, then reduce to a simmer, stirring to dissolve the sugar.
Continue to cook for 30 minutes, until the peel is transluscent.
Set aside to cool completely. Strain the syrup through a fine-
mesh sieve into a glass jar with a lid, cap tightly, and refrigerate.
The syrup will keep for 6 months.

To serve, pour the wine into tall glasses filled with ice and add a
dash of the orange syrup. Garnish each glass with an orange twist.

Tangerine 95

Tangerine

Tangerines have such playful and descriptive names, denoting subtle distinctions in sweetness, size, and color. At the farmers' market, you will often see hand-written signs proudly jutting out from a mound of beautiful orange balls with names like Yosemite Gold, Gold Nugget, Honey, Dancy, Pixie, and Page.

Tangerines are typically smaller, have looser, easier-to-peel skin, more delicate pith, and are less acidic—and thus sweeter—than oranges. In markets, you will often find the terms *tangerine* and *mandarin orange* used interchangeably for the same fruits. Tangerines have a long season, with the many different varieties popping up in markets from November through late spring.

When the markets are brimming with these fruits, take advantage of the bounty and buy them in bulk. Preserve them in salt (page 116) or bottle them in a sweet, sticky dessert wine (page 115). Or you can juice them, and freeze the juice in ice-cube trays, and then pop the cubes into an evening cocktail or into a glass of soda water for a citrusy flourish.

Satsumas and *clementines*, which originate in Japan and North Africa, are two of the most popular mandarin orange types, and are great favorites for eating by hand, as they are seedless and especially easy to peel.

Don't toss away that peel. Use it to make a favorite chemical-free kitchen cleaner of ours: Immerse the peels in distilled white vinegar in a large jar, let stand at room temperature for three weeks, and then strain and decant into a spray bottle. Dilute the mixture with water, or use it full strength for stubborn, greasy stains.

These crepes are the perfect way to start your morning, especially on the weekend when you can relax and take time to enjoy them. Any citrus works well here, but tangerines give a light and unexpected flavor. For a simple dessert, spread the crepes with Clementine Curd (page 108), roll them up, and dust them with confectioners' sugar.

BREAKFAST CREPES WITH CANDIED TANGERINES

~Makes 12 crepes

1 cup sugar

1 cup water

3 tangerines, thinly sliced

²/₃ cup all-purpose flour

1 egg

1 egg yolk

2 tablespoons unsalted butter, melted, plus more for cooking

³/₄ cup whole milk

In a saucepan, combine the sugar and water and bring to a boil over high heat, stirring to dissolve the sugar. Turn down the heat to medium and simmer, stirring occasionally, for 5 minutes, until the sugar has dissolved completely. Add the tangerines and continue to simmer for 8 to 10 minutes, until the fruit is translucent and the syrup has thickened. Remove from the heat, set aside, and let cool.

In a blender, combine the flour, egg, egg yolk, melted butter, and milk and blend until smooth. Cover and refrigerate for at least 1 hour or for up to overnight.

Place an 8-inch pan over medium-high heat, add a knob of butter, and swirl the pan to coat the bottom evenly. Ladle ¼ cup of the crepe batter into the hot pan and swirl the pan to coat the bottom evenly with batter. Cook for about 1 minute, until the batter is lightly browned on the bottom. Using a small metal spatula, lift the edge of the crepe and flip it over. Cook the other side until golden and brown.

Transfer to a warmed plate and repeat with the remaining batter. To serve, fold two crepes in half, place them on a plate, and spoon some candied tangerines on top.

Serve this lightly spiced flatbread as part of a mezze plate filled with *burrata* and a mix of olives. Use it to mop up the extra juices from a tagine or soup, or eat it as you would pita bread.

MOROCCAN FLATBREAD

~Makes 6 small breads

2 cups self-rising flour

4 preserved tangerine wedges (page 116)

3 tablespoons dried mint

1 cup hot water

1 tablespoon harissa

¼ cup olive oil

Burrata cheese, for serving

Ground sumac, for sprinkling

Olives, for serving

Put the flour in a large bowl. Rinse off the salt from the preserved tangerines under cold water. Remove and discard the flesh, and finely chop the skins. Add the skins and mint to the flour and stir well. Pour in the hot water, stir until the mixture comes together in a rough mass, and then form the dough into a ball.

Generously flour a work surface and transfer the dough to it. Divide the dough into 6 equal balls. Roll each ball into a circle about the size of your hand and ¼ inch thick.

In a small bowl, stir together the harissa and oil. Brush the mixture on top of each dough circle. Using a small, sharp knife, score an X on top of each bread, being careful not to cut all the way through.

Heat a stove-top grill pan over medium-high heat until smoking. Working in batches, place the breads oil side down on the hot pan. Cook for a few moments, until bubbles begin to appear on the surface of the dough. Turn the breads over and continue to cook for 3 to 4 minutes longer, until slightly charred and golden brown on the bottom. Repeat with the remaining breads. To serve, place on a platter with torn burrata sprinkled with the sumac and the olives.

When we were photographing this slaw and tucking in for lunch, we discovered that it goes amazingly well with the Tangerine Sticky Ribs (page 107). It will take you five minutes to put this dish together and it is the perfect picnic or camping food—so easy to transport.

FENNEL, TANGERINE & OLIVE SLAW

~Serves 4 to 6

1 fennel bulb with fronds attached

1 Granny Smith apple

4 tangerines, peeled and thinly sliced

¼ cup sliced green olives

VINAIGRETTE

Zest and juice of
1 tangerine

2 pinches red pepper flakes

1 teaspoon honey

1 teaspoon whole-grain Dijon mustard

2 teaspoons sherry vinegar

¼ cup extra virgin olive oil

Sea salt and freshly cracked black pepper

Fennel blossoms, for garnish (optional)

Cut the fennel fronds from the fennel and set aside. Using a mandoline or a sharp knife, cut the fennel bulb into matchsticks and transfer to a large serving bowl. Cut the apple the same way and add to the fennel. Add the tangerine slices and toss in the olives.

To make the vinaigrette, combine all of the ingredients in a glass jar with a tight fitting lid. Screw the lid on and shake the jar vigorously until the mixture emulsifies.

Pour the vinaigrette over the slaw and toss to mix thoroughly. Season with salt and pepper and toss again. Cover and refrigerate for 1 hour.

To serve, tear the fronds and sprinkle them and the fennel blossoms on top of the slaw.

The smokiness of the jalapeños and the sweetness of the tangerines bathe these scallops with explosive flavors. If you like, serve them on a bed of crisp greens, or on couscous for something a little heartier, and pour a chilled white wine.

PANFRIED SCALLOPS WITH SMOKY JALAPEÑO & TANGERINE RELISH

~Serves 4

RELISH

4 jalapeño chiles

1 tangerine, peeled

¼ cup finely chopped shallot

Juice of 1 tangerine

2 tablespoons clear honey

Sea salt and freshly ground black pepper

12 diver sea scallops

Coarse sea salt and freshly cracked black pepper

Smoked paprika

2 tablespoons olive oil

To make the relish, place a cast-iron or other heavy sauté pan over high heat until smoking. Add the chiles and cook, turning as needed, until the skins are charred on all sides. Remove from the heat, allow to cool slightly, then coarsely chop and place in a bowl.

Coarsely chop the tangerine, then add it and the shallot to the chiles and stir to mix. In a small bowl, whisk together the tangerine juice and honey and pour over the chile-tangerine mixture. Season with salt and pepper and set aside.

Season the scallops on both sides with salt and pepper and sprinkle lightly with smoked paprika.

Return the pan to medium-high heat. When the pan is hot, add the oil, then swirl the pan to coat the bottom evenly. Add the scallops and cook, turning once with tongs, for 1 to 2 minutes on each side, until golden brown on both sides and still slightly translucent at the center.

Transfer the scallops to a platter, top with the relish, and serve immediately.

Each bite into these perfectly grilled drumettes—doused in sweet mandarin juice and honey and with a little spice from the mustard—will make you want to take another. They can be cooked on a stove-top grill pan or charcoal grill and are great finger food for backyard get-togethers.

GRILLED HONEY MANDARIN CHICKEN DRUMETTES

~Serves 4 to 6

12 chicken drumettes

Sea salt and freshly ground black pepper

Grated zest and juice of 1 mandarin orange

¼ cup orange blossom honey

2 tablespoons olive oil

1 tablespoon Dijon mustard

Place the drumettes in a large bowl and season with salt and pepper.

In a small bowl, whisk together the mandarin zest and juice, honey, oil, and mustard, mixing well. Pour the mixture over the chicken, then toss the drumettes until they are completely coated. Cover and refrigerate for at least 3 hours or up to overnight.

Remove the chicken from the refrigerator and bring to room temperature.

Heat a stove-top grill pan over medium-high until smoking. Remove the drumettes from the marinade, reserving the marinade, and arrange the drumettes in a single layer in the hot pan. Cook for about 5 minutes, until golden brown. Turn the drumettes over, reduce the heat to medium, and cook for another 5 minutes, making sure all sides are brown and cooked through.

While the drumettes are cooking, pour the reserved marinade into a small saucepan, place over high heat, bring to a boil, and boil for about 5 minutes, until reduced to a thick sauce.

Remove the drumettes from the heat and pile them high on a serving platter. Pour the sauce over the top and serve immediately.

Except for the time in the oven, everything for this quick-and-easy recipe happens in a blender. And don't miss the freshly chopped tangerine peel garnish to zest things up. These ribs are so finger-lickin' good that they enticed Victoria to eat meat again!

TANGERINE STICKY RIBS

~Serves 4 to 6

1 rack baby back pork ribs, about 3 pounds

4 to 6 star anise pods

MARINADE

Peels from 2 tangerines, coarsely chopped

1 cup orange blossom honey

¼ cup hoisin sauce

¼ cup toasted sesame oil

1 large clove garlic, coarsely chopped

1 (2-inch) knob fresh ginger, peeled and coarsely chopped

1 teaspoon Szechuan peppercorns

1 teaspoon Chinese five-spice powder

1 tablespoon sambal oelek

2 tablespoons chopped tangerine peel, for garnish

Rinse the ribs under cold water and pat dry with a paper towel. Place the ribs in a baking dish, sprinkle with the star anise, and set aside.

To make the marinade, in a blender, combine all of the ingredients and process until the mixture is fairly smooth. Pour over the ribs, cover tightly with aluminum foil, and refrigerate overnight.

Preheat the oven to 300°F. Remove the ribs from the refrigerator and bring to room temperature, about 30 minutes. Place the covered dish in the oven and cook for 2½ hours.

Remove the ribs from the oven. Remove the foil and set aside. Baste the ribs with the sauce and return to the oven, uncovered. Cook for another 30 minutes.

Remove the ribs from the oven and tent with the reserved foil. Allow to rest for 15 minutes. Transfer the rack to a cutting board and cut between the bones. Serve with a sprinkle of tangerine peel.

Clementines make a wonderfully tangy curd that can be used in so many ways: served alongside scones and breads, used to fill tarts and crepes (page 99), spread between layers of sponge cake, spooned atop ice cream, or swirled through crème fraîche for accompanying pound cake.

CLEMENTINE CURD

~Makes about 1 cup

6 egg yolks

¼ cup sugar

Zest of 2 clementines

½ cup freshly squeezed clementine juice

1 teaspoon freshly squeezed lemon juice

½ cup unsalted butter, cut into small cubes

In a heatproof bowl, whisk together the egg yolks, sugar, clementine zest and juice, and lemon juice just until blended. Place the bowl over (not touching) simmering water in a saucepan and continue to whisk constantly for 6 to 8 minutes, until the mixture has thickened.

Remove from the heat and whisk in the butter cubes one at time.

Pour the warm curd into a sterilized jar and allow to cool. Cap tightly and store in the refrigerator for up to 1 week.

These chocolate-dipped treats are a sweet way to end dinner. They also make lovely gifts. Add a couple of dried chiles to the syrup to make them both spicy and sweet. The leftover syrup can be stored in the refrigerator for up to 3 months and used for making sorbets or as a sweetener in teas or cocktails.

CANDIED CHOCOLATE MANDARINS

~*Makes about 24 slices*

4½ cups sugar

2 cups water

6 firm, ripe mandarin oranges, sliced crosswise into ¼-inch-thick pieces

½ cup sugar

10 ounces good-quality dark chocolate (preferably 70% cocoa), chopped

In a saucepan, combine 4 cups of the sugar and the water and bring to a boil over high heat, stirring constantly, until the sugar has dissolved completely, about 5 minutes.

Reduce the heat to low, add the mandarin slices, and simmer until translucent, about 20 minutes, pushing the fruit gently down with a wooden spoon to make sure the slices are submerged. Remove the pan from the heat and let cool completely, about 1 hour.

Place a wire rack over a sheet pan. Using tongs, remove the slices, shaking off any excess syrup. Place on the rack in a single layer. Let the slices dry overnight. Reserve the syrup for another use.

The next day, spread the remaining ½ cup of sugar on a small plate. Toss the dried mandarin slices with the sugar to coat evenly, then return them to the wire rack in a single layer.

Line a baking sheet with parchment paper. Put the chocolate in a heatproof bowl placed over simmering water in a saucepan. Melt the chocolate, stirring until smooth. Remove from the heat.

Dip each sugared mandarin slice halfway into the chocolate and then place on the parchment in a single layer. Leave until the chocolate has set, about 1 hour. The slices can be stored in an airtight container at room temperature for up to 1 week.

This is a lovely twist on the beloved lemon meringue pie. Mandarin oranges make a sweet, floral filling that begs to be eaten warm—maybe with a dollop of crème fraîche.

MANDARIN MERINGUE TART

~Serves 8

TART DOUGH

2 cups all-purpose flour

¾ cup cold unsalted butter, cut into small cubes

Pinch of sea salt

1 egg, lightly beaten

5 tablespoons ice water

FILLING

3 tablespoons cornstarch

1 cup freshly squeezed mandarin orange juice

1 cup water

Zest of 1 mandarin orange

3 tablespoons superfine sugar

4 egg yolks

MERINGUE

4 egg whites

¾ cup superfine sugar

To make the tart dough, in a food processor, pulse the flour, butter, and salt until the mixture looks like bread crumbs. With the motor running, add the egg and then the water, 1 tablespoon at a time, until the dough comes together.

Turn the dough out onto a lightly floured surface and knead into a disc. Cover with plastic wrap and refrigerate for 30 minutes.

Butter a 10-inch tart pan with a removable bottom. Remove the dough from the refrigerator and transfer it to a lightly floured surface. Roll it into a 12-inch circle, then ease it into the prepared pan, gently pressing it onto the bottom and sides. Trim the excess dough by rolling the pin over the top of the pan. Prick the base all over with a fork and cover with plastic wrap. Refrigerate for another 30 minutes. Meanwhile, preheat the oven to 375°F.

Remove the tart shell from the refrigerator, line it with parchment paper, and fill it with pie weights. Bake for 15 minutes, until dry to the touch, then remove the weights and parchment and bake for a further 10 minutes. Transfer the pan to a wire rack. Reduce the oven temperature to 275°F.

To make the filling, in a saucepan over medium heat, whisk together the cornstarch, mandarin orange juice, water, and zest, until it thickens. Remove from the heat and whisk in the sugar and then the egg yolks. Pour the mixture into the tart shell.

To make the meringue, using a stand mixer fitted with the whisk attachment, beat the egg whites on high speed until soft white peaks form. Add a third of the sugar at a time and continue to beat until stiff, glossy peaks have formed.

Using a spatula, spoon the meringue over the filling and spread it to the edge of the tart shell. Make a few decorative swirls in the meringue, then bake the pie for 30 to 35 minutes, until the meringue is golden and set. Transfer to a wire rack and serve warm or at room temperature.

This is one of our favorite ways to eat satsumas. Enjoy them straight from the jar with lashings of heavy cream. This recipe also works with other citrus fruits and with other spices and herbs. I first pack the fruit into the prepared jars to determine how many I will need to use; sometimes I just use one really large glass jar.

SATSUMAS IN SWEET WINE

~Makes 12 satsumas

12 small satsumas

1 or more cinnamon sticks (optional)

1 (750 ml) bottle sweet white dessert wine (such as Muscat)

Peel the satsumas, removing as much of the stringy pith as possible. Reserve the peels for another use.

Pack the fruits into sterilized jars, leaving ½ inch of headspace. Slide a cinnamon stick down the side of each jar, then pour in the wine to cover the fruits. Screw on the lid(s) and store in a cool, dark place for 2 to 3 months before using. Once opened, they will keep in the refrigerator for up to 3 months.

You can preserve other citrus besides lemon and limes—
including tangerines. Use this pantry staple for all types of
dishes: sprinkled on pizza, stirred through rice, or added
to soups and stews. Make it in one large glass jar or a few
smaller ones to give to friends.

PRESERVED TANGERINES

~Makes 1 quart

6 tangerines

1 cup sea salt

1 tablespoon mixed
peppercorns (such as
white, pink, black, and
green)

1½ cups freshly squeezed
tangerine juice

Cut the tangerines into quarters or sixths, depending on
their size.

Pour 2 tablespoons of the salt onto the bottom of a sterilized
1-quart jar and top with a layer of tangerine wedges. Sprinkle
a few peppercorns on top and continue to fill the jar with
alternating layers of salt, tangerine wedges, and peppercorns.
Pack the fruit down as you go and finish with a layer of salt and
a scattering of peppercorns. Pour the tangerine juice into the jar.
If the tangerines aren't covered by juice, add water to cover.

Screw on the lid tightly and store in the refrigerator for 1 month
before using. They will keep for up to 6 months longer. To use the
tangerines, rinse off the salt under cold running water, remove
and discard the flesh, and use the skins as desired.

Traditionally, this cocktail is made with lime, but here tangerines give a deep, sweet flavor that works especially well with the rum. This is the perfect drink for a hot summer evening—colorful, cooling, and bursting with flavor.

TANGERINE DAIQUIRI

~Serves 2

2 tangerines, peeled and coarsely chopped

4 ounces white rum

1½ ounces Cointreau

1 teaspoon superfine sugar

1 cup ice

Have ready 2 chilled glasses. In a blender, combine all of the ingredients and blend until smooth. Divide between the 2 glasses and serve.

Devilishly refreshing and so pretty, this combination of sweet, bright orange Page tangerine juice and deep red, pleasantly bitter Campari sings out. Make this as soon as possible for your new sundowner.

PAGE TANGERINE NEGRONI

~Serves 2

4 ounces freshly squeezed Page tangerine juice (about 3 fruits)

2 ounces Hendrick's gin

2 ounces Campari

2 ounces Carpano Antica sweet vermouth

Ice, for cocktail shaker

2 Page tangerine slices

Have ready 2 chilled cocktail glasses. Pour the tangerine juice, gin, Campari, and vermouth into a cocktail shaker filled with ice. Cover, shake vigorously, and then strain into the glasses. Garnish each drink with a tangerine slice and serve.

Grapefruit | 121

Grapefruit

The majestic grapefruit brings a smile to all. The name *grapefruit* comes from the way the fruits grow in hanging clusters like enormous grapes. Grapefruits vary in shape, size, and acidity, and also in color, which makes them fun to cook with or to eat as is.

You can peel and slice two or three different types of grapefruit to make a beautiful citrus salad. You can sprinkle halves with sugar and broil, as we do in Burnt Cinnamon-Sugar Grapefruit (page 129). You can use their juice and zest for a creamy sauce for scallops (page 137), or stuff them in roasted pork loin (page 136).

Grapefruit types are defined by the color of their flesh: yellow (aka white), pink, and ruby. Among the yellow clan is the *Oroblanco*. The *Rex Union*, a hybrid of the pleasantly sour Seville orange and the pomelo, has pale orange flesh, a tangy flavor, and a thick peel, perfect for marmalades and candying. The *Cocktail*, a hybrid of the pomelo and a mandarin orange, has dark yellow-orange flesh, is smaller and sweeter than the average grapefruit, and has a lot of seeds, which means it's good for juicing.

The pink varieties, such as *Ray Ruby*, *Marsh Pink*, and *Redblush*, boast light yellow flesh with a subtle rose blush. These fruits tend to be juicier and sweeter than yellow grapefruits. The ruby group, including the *Rio Red*, *Star Ruby*, and *Rio Star*, has light to deep red flesh that adds a beautiful splash of color to nearly any dish and makes a great marmalade, especially laced with gin (page 125).

The *pomelo*, the largest of all of the citrus fruits, is a native of South Asia and Southeast Asia. It has a mild, sweet flavor, making it a good choice for sauces or salads. Its thick peel, which is pale green to yellow when the fruit is ripe, is great for marmalades and candying.

The sweet perfumed taste and thick skins of ruby grapefruits make them ideal for marmalade. The addition of the gin gives the marmalade a deep, tangy flavor.

GRAPEFRUIT & GIN MARMALADE

~Makes about 5¹⁄₂ pints

4 ruby grapefruits, about 5 pounds total weight

4 quarts water

8 cups superfine sugar (3 ¹⁄₂ pounds)

Zest and juice of 1 lemon

¹⁄₄ cup Hendrick's gin

Place a small plate in the freezer. Wash the grapefruits thoroughly and cut them into quarters. Line a fine-mesh sieve with a piece of cheesecloth large enough to overlap the edges and place the sieve over a bowl to catch the juices.

Squeeze the grapefruit wedges into the sieve to release the juices, then scrape out the flesh with a spoon, leaving a clean peel. Tie the corners of the cheesecloth into a knot and squeeze out any excess juice into the bowl; set aside.

Using a sharp knife, cut each cleaned peel in half lengthwise and then cut crosswise into thick or thin shreds, depending on your preference.

Put the sliced peel and cheesecloth in a preserving pan or other large, nonreactive pan and pour in the water and reserved juice. Bring to a boil over medium-high heat. Turn down the heat to medium-low and simmer uncovered, stirring occasionally, for 2 hours.

Remove the cheesecloth, squeeze as much of the liquid as possible back into the pan with a pair of tongs, and discard

continued

GRAPEFRUIT & GIN MARMALADE
continued

the cheesecloth. Add the sugar, lemon zest and juice, and gin to the pan, raise the heat to high, and bring to a boil, stirring continuously until the sugar dissolves. Boil for 10 minutes.

At this point, the bubbles should be small and the mixture should begin to look dense. Remove the chilled plate from the freezer, drop a small spoonful of the marmalade onto it, and return it to the freezer for 2 to 3 minutes. Pull it from the freezer and check the texture. The dollop should be thick and syrupy, not runny. If not thick, boil the marmalade for another 10 minutes and test again. Repeat until you have the desired consistency. It can take up to 30 minutes to reach the setting point. Stir the marmalade occasionally to make sure it is not sticking to the bottom of the pan. (Alternatively, you can test the marmalade with a candy thermometer, which should register 220°F when ready.)

Once the marmalade has reached setting point, remove the pan from the heat and let the marmalade rest for 10 minutes. This helps to ensure that the beautiful sliced peel is suspended evenly throughout the marmalade, rather than sitting on the bottom of the canning jars. Using a large spoon, skim off any scum from the surface, as it can make the marmalade cloudy.

Preheat the oven to 250°F. Pour the marmalade into warm sterilized jars, leaving ½ inch of space. Screw the lids on. Wipe the jars clean and place them in a baking dish. Place in the preheated oven for 25 minutes to seal.

Remove the jars from the oven and set on a cooling rack. Leave undisturbed until they have cooled completely. You will hear a ping sound as each lids seals. Check to make sure that the center of the lid is concave. Store the jars in a cool, dark cupboard for up to 1 year. If a seal is not good, store the jar in the refrigerator and use within 3 weeks.

Victoria's garden is full of grapefruit trees, among other citrus, and this is one of her favorite ways to eat them. Broiled until the cinnamon-sugar topping caramelizes, the grapefruits are served warm and sweet. Offer them at breakfast or brunch or as a quick dessert for a weeknight get-together.

BURNT CINNAMON-SUGAR GRAPEFRUIT

~Serves 4

2 ruby grapefruits or 1 pomelo, halved crosswise

¼ cup turbinado sugar

1 teaspoon ground cinnamon

Honey, for drizzling

Preheat the broiler to high.

Arrange the grapefruit halves in a baking dish, cut side up. In a small bowl, stir together the sugar and cinnamon, then evenly sprinkle the mixture over the tops of the grapefruit halves. Drizzle with a little honey.

Place under the boiler and cook for 6 to 8 minutes, until the sugar has caramelized. Serve at once.

This aioli, which has a sweet-tart citrus flavor from the addition of both pomelo juice and zest, is ideal for dipping fresh raw vegetables. It is also delicious spread on toasted burger buns or dolloped on grilled meats and fish.

CRUDITÉS WITH POMELO AIOLI

~Makes about 1 cup aioli

AIOLI

2 egg yolks

1 clove garlic, smashed

1/2 teaspoon Dijon mustard

2 tablespoons freshly squeezed pomelo juice

1 cup olive oil

Grated zest of 1 pomelo

Sea salt and freshly ground black pepper

Handfuls of cherry tomatoes, green beans, radishes, and celery, in any combination

To make the aioli, in a food processor, combine the egg yolks, garlic, mustard, and pomelo juice and process until smooth. With the motor running, slowly add the oil, a few drops at a time in the beginning. When the mixture begins to emulsify and thicken, add the remaining oil in a slow, steady stream until all of it has been incorporated and the aioli is thick. Scrape out the aioli into a bowl, stir in the pomelo zest, and season with salt and pepper. Cover and refrigerate until ready to use.

Trim the vegetables as needed and arrange them on a platter. Spoon the aioli into a bowl alongside, and serve immediately.

The delicate, sweet flavor of the ruby grapefruit is hit with a dazzle of heat from Szechuan peppercorns, which are a delightful peppery spice used in Chinese cooking. You will find them in the spice rack at your local market; use them whole or grind them up as I've done here.

SZECHUAN SHRIMP & RUBY GRAPEFRUIT SALAD

~Serves 4

1 pound medium shrimp, peeled, with tails on

6 ounces dried vermicelli rice noodles

1 large ruby grapefruit, peeled

1 cup torn mint leaves

DRESSING

¼ cup honey

¼ cup freshly squeezed grapefruit juice

2 tablespoons toasted sesame oil

1 tablespoon fish sauce

½ teaspoon ground Szechuan peppercorns

Bring a saucepan filled with water to a boil over high heat. Add the shrimp and cook for 3 to 5 minutes, until they are opaque and cooked through. Drain and place in a large ceramic bowl.

Place the noodles in a heatproof bowl and pour in boiling water to cover. Let stand for 10 minutes, until soft, then drain and rinse under cool running water. Add to the shrimp.

Cut the grapefruit into segments and add them and any juices to the bowl with the shrimp and noodles. Add the mint leaves.

To make the dressing, in a small bowl, whisk together all of the ingredients. Pour over the salad, toss gently to coat evenly, and serve at once.

This is such a pretty salad—deep green kale, light green avocado, pale yellow grapefruit. It is perfect for lunch or supper.

YELLOW GRAPEFRUIT & AVOCADO SALAD

~Serves 4

1 yellow grapefruit, peeled

1 avocado, halved, pitted, peeled, and sliced

2 cups baby kale or similar greens

VINAIGRETTE

¼ cup extra virgin olive oil

2 tablespoons sherry vinegar

1 teaspoon Dijon mustard

3 tablespoons chopped tarragon

Sea salt and freshly ground black pepper

Quarter the grapefruit, then cut into ¼-inch slices. Arrange on a platter or in a shallow bowl. Top with the avocado slices, then sprinkle with the baby kale.

To make the vinaigrette, in a small bowl, whisk together the oil, vinegar, mustard, and tarragon. Season with salt and pepper.

Pour the vinaigrette over the salad and serve.

This is the most wonderful weekend meal. It takes no time to put together, and the oven does the rest, leaving you free to spend time with your guests. The earthy flavor of the fennel and tart-sweet taste of the grapefruit mingle together to infuse the pork, which is covered with crispy, salty prosciutto.

PROSCIUTTO ROASTED PORK LOIN STUFFED WITH GRAPEFRUIT

~Serves 4 to 6

2 tablespoons olive oil

1 cup finely chopped fennel

2 teaspoons ground fennel

1 yellow grapefruit, peeled and coarsely chopped

Sea salt and freshly cracked black pepper

1 (3-pound) boneless pork loin, butterflied

8 slices prosciutto

1 cup dry white wine

Preheat the oven to 425°F.

In a sauté pan, heat the oil over medium-high heat. Add the chopped fennel and cook, stirring often, for about 5 minutes, until tender and golden brown. Stir in the ground fennel, then remove from the heat. Add the chopped grapefruit, season with salt and pepper, and stir to combine.

Lay the pork, fat side down, on a work surface and season with salt and pepper. Spread the filling evenly over the pork, leaving a border about 1/2 inch wide. Starting from the edge nearest you, roll up the pork and place seam side down on the work surface. Wrap the prosciutto slices evenly around the pork, then secure the roast with butcher's twine tied at 1-inch intervals.

Place the roast in a small roasting pan or baking dish and pour the wine into the bottom of the pan. Roast for about 45 minutes, until an instant-read thermometer inserted into the center of the roast registers 140°F.

Remove from the oven, tent with aluminum foil, and let rest for 15 minutes. Carve the roast into thick slices, arrange on a platter, and serve.

Here, we bathe large sweet scallops in a perfumed cream with a light, bright citrus flavor. They're especially good on top of a pile of fresh rustic pasta.

SCALLOPS WITH OROBLANCO CREAM

-Serves 2

6 diver sea scallops

Coarse sea salt and freshly ground black pepper

1 tablespoon olive oil

Zest and juice of
1 Oroblanco grapefruit

¼ cup crème fraîche

¼ cup torn basil leaves

Season the scallops on both sides with salt and pepper.

Place a cast-iron or other heavy frying pan over medium-high heat. When the pan is hot, add the oil, then swirl the pan to coat the bottom evenly. Add the scallops and cook, turning once with tongs, for 1 to 2 minutes on each side, until golden brown on both sides and still slightly translucent at the center. Transfer the scallops to a warmed plate.

With the pan still over medium-high heat, add the grapefruit zest and juice and deglaze the pan. Stir in the crème fraîche and cook for 2 minutes. Remove from the heat.

Divide the scallops evenly between 2 plates and spoon the sauce over the top. Garnish with the basil and serve at once.

Whenever I visit Victoria and it's grapefruit season, I seem to come home with far more than I need. The trees are always full of plump fruit begging to be picked. After making marmalade and candied peel, then eating them just as they are, I like to make granita and add herbs, like basil or mint. It is always a refreshing way to end a meal.

POMELO & BASIL GRANITA

~Serves 6

½ cup sugar

½ cup water

2½ cups freshly squeezed pomelo juice

½ cup tightly packed basil leaves or mint leaves

In a small saucepan, combine the sugar and water over medium-high heat and bring to a boil, stirring to dissolve the sugar. Turn down the heat to medium and simmer, stirring occasionally, for 5 minutes, until the sugar has dissolved completely.

Pour the sugar syrup into a blender, add the pomelo juice and basil, and puree for about 30 seconds, until the basil appears as specks in the mixture. Pour into a shallow baking dish and freeze until solid.

To serve, run a fork through the frozen sheet to break it up into large crystals, then spoon the crystals into small bowls.

The mild, fragrant pomelo is also known as the Chinese grapefruit or the shaddock, after the sea captain who introduced this mighty fruit to the West Indies. These delightfully creamy possets are perfumed with the pomelo's zest and juice and topped with its sharp sugary peel.

POMELO POSSETS WITH CANDIED PEEL

~Serves 6

2 cups heavy cream

²/₃ cup sugar

Zest of 1 pomelo

6 tablespoons freshly squeezed pomelo juice

Candied pomelo or grapefruit peel (page 165), for garnish

In a saucepan, combine the cream and sugar and bring to a boil over medium heat, stirring to dissolve the sugar. Turn down the heat to low, add the zest, and simmer, stirring occasionally, for 5 minutes. Be careful not to let the cream boil over.

Remove from the heat, stir in the grapefruit juice, and let stand for 10 minutes.

Pour the mixture into 4 small cups or bowls and cool completely, then cover and refrigerate overnight.

Just before serving, garnish each bowl with the candied peel.

And the Rest · 143

And the Rest

This chapter sums up the wonderful, quirky, and slightly out-of-the-ordinary citrus that can be found at your local markets. These are always fun in color, shape, and taste. Squeeze, zest, and cut the fruits into wonderful shapes for garnishing and flavoring everything from salads to a party cocktail.

The *citron,* a large, aromatic citrus fruit native to Asia, is prized for its thick skin. The showiest member of the group is the *Buddha's hand,* also known as fingered citron, which has slender, finger like segments. You can candy the peel, infuse gin or vodka, or use the zest for sauces or batters. Just one of these gems will perfume a room for days.

Like the Buddha's hand, *yuzu* is highly aromatic and has thick skin. Reminiscent of a cross between an orange and a lime, this small fruit has some flesh, many seeds, and relatively little juice. While it's hard to find fresh, you can buy bottled yuzu juice at Japanese and other Asian markets and some specialty markets. You can zest the skin and stir it through sweet or savory dishes, such as rice (page 151), or juice them and enjoy the tart, fragrant nectar in a cocktail or sauce.

Kumquats, in contrast, are more readily available in stores and farmers' markets. They're also very easy to grow in pots. Brimming with floral, tart flavors, the little torpedo-shaped fruits can be eaten as is, although you will encounter a few seeds. You can turn kumquats into butters, salts, or oils, or bathe them in sugar syrup and serve them with ice cream or alongside rich, dark meats.

Many of the recipes in this chapter call for one of these three quirky fruits, but we have also included basic recipes that can be made with different types of citrus, from salt and oil to butter and dried sugared slices. Stock your pantry with some of these staples—you'll find yourself turning to them again and again for a burst of citrus flavor.

Whipping up this butter is quick and so simple. Use it as is or mix in a favorite spice or herb and then toss with hot rice or pasta. For a morning treat, mix it with honey or maple syrup and top your pancakes or waffles or spread it on freshly baked scones. For a grown-up version, add a splash of your favorite liqueur along with the citrus.

KUMQUAT BUTTER

~Makes about 1¹/₂ cups

12 kumquats or the equivalent amount of another citrus

1 cup salted butter, at room temperature

In a food processor, combine the kumquats and butter and process until smooth.

At this point, you can either transfer the butter to an airtight container or form it into a roll. To shape a butter roll, place a piece of plastic wrap on a work surface and scrape the butter onto the wrap, then fold the sides of the wrap around the butter and roll it into a log.

The butter will keep in the refrigerator for up to 1 week or in the freezer for up to 3 months.

Opening the parchment-paper packet that encloses this salmon is like receiving a gift from the sea—a bouquet of irresistible aromas. If you can't find yuzu juice, flavor the salmon with lemon or lime juice. Wild salmon is always our first choice, but if you cannot find it, use sustainable farm-raised salmon.

YUZU-GLAZED SALMON

~Serves 4

2 tablespoons freshly squeezed or bottled yuzu juice

1 tablespoon yellow miso

1 tablespoon soy sauce

2 tablespoons maple syrup

2 heads baby bok choy, trimmed and sliced lengthwise

1 (2-pound) skinless center-cut wild salmon fillet

1 tablespoon sesame seeds

Preheat the oven to 425°F. Cut out a square of parchment paper about three times larger than the salmon fillet.

In a small bowl, whisk together the yuzu juice, miso, soy sauce, and maple syrup.

Lay the parchment paper on a sheet pan. Arrange the bok choy on the right half of the paper, leaving a 2-inch border uncovered on all sides. Place the salmon on top of the bok choy, drizzle with the yuzu mixture, then sprinkle with the sesame seeds.

Take the left-hand side of the parchment and fold it over the salmon. Pleat the edges together to form a parcel, sealing the fish tightly in the packet. Check to make sure there are no gaps along the edges.

Place in the oven and bake for 25 minutes. The salmon should be cooked through and just tender at the center.

Remove from the oven and let rest for a few minutes. Cut the packet open, divide the salmon and bok choy among plates, and drizzle with some of the cooking juices.

Bright orange kumquats cooked up in a thick syrupy sauce and then drizzled over grilled duck breasts is a feast to remember and deserves center stage at any table. Serve with Citrus Japanese Rice (page 151) and enjoy.

GRILLED DUCK WITH GINGER KUMQUATS

~Serves 4

¼ cup mirin

¼ cup tamari

1 tablespoon Dijon mustard

4 (8-ounce) duck breasts

3 tablespoons dark brown sugar

2 tablespoons cider vinegar

12 kumquats, halved and seeds removed

1 fresh red chile, minced (about 2 tablespoons)

1 (2-inch) knob fresh ginger, peeled and grated

In a small bowl, whisk together the mirin, tamari, and mustard. Put the duck breasts, skin side up, in a glass or ceramic dish, and pour the mirin mixture evenly over the top. Cover and set aside at room temperature for 1 hour.

To make the sauce, in a saucepan, combine the sugar and vinegar and bring to a boil over high heat, stirring to dissolve the sugar. Turn down the heat to medium and simmer, stirring constantly, until the sugar has dissolved. Add the kumquats, chile, and ginger and continue to simmer, stirring often, for 8 to 10 minutes, until syrupy. Remove from the heat and set aside.

Place a large stove-top grill pan over high heat until smoking. Remove the duck breasts from the marinade and place them, skin side down, on the hot pan. Discard the marinade. Cook the duck breasts for 6 minutes, then turn the breasts over, turn the heat down to medium, and cook for 6 minutes longer. The breasts should be medium-rare and pink inside.

Transfer the duck to a cutting board, tent with aluminum foil, and let rest for 5 minutes.

Slice the duck breasts against the grain, place them on plates or in bowls, and top with the kumquats.

This is one of my go-to dishes. Laced with tart, lemony yuzu and sweet mirin, it makes a wonderful citrus rice bowl that I top with grilled meats and fish. I always make extra, so the next day I can toss it into a smoking hot wok along with a couple of eggs for fragrant fried rice.

CITRUS JAPANESE RICE

-Serves 4 to 6

2 cups sushi rice

2 cups water

Zest and juice of 1 yuzu, or 4 tablespoons bottled yuzu juice

3 tablespoons mirin

2 tablespoons toasted sesame seeds

4 green onions, white and green parts, finely chopped

Rinse the rice under cold running water until the water runs clear.

In a saucepan, combine the rice and the water and bring to a boil over high heat. Cover, turn down the heat to low, and cook for 20 minutes, until the water has been absorbed and the rice is tender. Remove from the heat and let rest, covered, for 10 minutes.

In a small bowl, whisk together the yuzu zest and juice, mirin, and sesame seeds.

Uncover the rice, pour the yuzu sauce over the rice, and then stir until completely mixed.

Transfer to a serving bowl, top with the green onions, and serve at once.

Dainty, tart kumquat slices in maple syrup sit perfectly on these rich chocolate waffles and make a playful dessert. You can make the maple kumquats a day ahead, so you have more time for waffle making.

DARK CHOCOLATE WAFFLES WITH MAPLE KUMQUATS

~Serves 6

KUMQUATS

18 kumquats

1 cup maple syrup

WAFFLE BATTER

1 1/2 cups all-purpose flour

2 tablespoons dark brown sugar

1 teaspoon baking powder

1/2 teaspoon baking soda

Pinch of salt

1/2 cup Dutch-processed cocoa powder

2 cups buttermilk, at room temperature

3 eggs, at room temperature

2 tablespoons unsalted butter, melted and cooled

1/4 cup chopped dark chocolate (70% cacao), melted and cooled

To make the kumquats, slice them thinly, discarding any seeds. In a small saucepan, add the maple syrup and kumquats and bring to a simmer over medium heat. Cook for 6 to 8 minutes, until the kumquats release their oils and juices. Remove from the heat and set aside. (If made ahead, cover and set aside at room temperature for up to 24 hours.)

Preheat a waffle iron according to the manufacturer's directions and spray with nonstick cooking spray.

To make the waffle batter, in a blender, combine the flour, sugar, baking powder, baking soda, salt, and cocoa powder and blend briefly to mix. Add the buttermilk, eggs, butter, and chocolate and blend just until combined. Do not overmix. Let rest for 10 minutes.

Pour about 1/2 cup of the batter into each waffle compartment, close the lid, and cook for 3 to 4 minutes, until golden brown. Transfer the waffles onto a plate, cover with a kitchen towel to keep warm, and repeat with the remaining batter.

To serve, place a waffle on each plate and pour the maple kumquats over.

Homemade candied citron is much better than anything you can buy at the store, which doesn't normally have much taste. Dip these sugared Buddha's hand pieces—or use another type of citron—in dark chocolate, chop them up to use as garnish, or stir them into cookie doughs or cake batters.

CANDIED CITRON

~Makes about 1 cup

1 Buddha's hand

3 cups sugar, plus more to coat

3 cups water

1/2 teaspoon baking soda

Wash and dry the Buddha's hand and cut into 1/4-inch pieces or slices 1/4 inch thick.

Place the fruit in a saucepan, cover with cold water, and bring to a simmer over medium-low heat. Continue to cook for 45 minutes.

Drain the fruit and set aside. In the same saucepan, combine the sugar and water and bring to a boil over medium-high heat, stirring to dissolve the sugar. Turn down the heat to medium and simmer, stirring occasionally, for about 5 minutes.

Add the baking soda and stir well. Add the reserved fruit, adjust the heat so the syrup is barely simmering, and cook for 45 minutes, until the fruit is translucent.

Have ready a wire rack set over a sheet of parchment paper. Using a slotted spoon, remove the fruit from the pan, shaking off any excess syrup, and spread it in a single layer on the rack. Let the peel dry at room temperature overnight. The next day, spread some sugar on a sheet pan and roll the peel in the sugar to coat. Store the peel in an airtight container at room temperature for up to 3 months.

The dash of yuzu juice gives a gentle tang to this sparkling aperitif. Serve it for weekend brunches or at the beginning of an evening meal. Sugaring the rim adds a dash of glamour that's never amiss with cocktails.

YUZU COCKTAIL

~Serves 4

Zest of 1 tangerine

2 tablespoons sugar

4 ounces freshly squeezed tangerine juice, well chilled

2 ounces freshly squeezed or bottled yuzu juice

1 (750 ml) bottle Prosecco, well chilled

Chill 4 champagne flutes or other stemmed cocktail glasses in the freezer. On a small plate, mix together the tangerine zest and sugar.

Run a piece of tangerine peel (left over from juicing) around the rim of each glass, dampening it. Then invert each glass onto the sugar to lightly rim the edge.

Divide the tangerine juice evenly among the prepared glasses, then add ½ ounce of the yuzu juice to each glass. Top up each glass with the chilled Prosecco and serve.

Flavored salts are usually expensive, but luckily they're a breeze to make. You can use more than one type of zest for each batch of salt, add a spice or dried herbs, or try different salts, such as smoked, pink, or gray, to come up with your own unique collection of citrus salts.

CITRUS SALT

~Makes ¹/₂ cup

¹/₂ cup flaky sea salt

3 tablespoons citrus zest, any kind

In a small bowl, combine the salt and citrus zest and mix well with your fingertips. (You can also use a mortar and pestle.) You want to release as much of the natural oils from the zest as possible.

Spread the mixture evenly on a plate and let dry at room temperature overnight. Transfer to a glass container with a tight-fitting lid and store at room temperature for up to 3 months.

Select a fruity high-quality olive oil to complement the flavorful zest, then use the citrusy oil in salad dressings, drizzled over grilled foods, or as a dip for crusty breads.

CITRUS OIL

~Makes 1 cup

3 limes, 1 orange, 1 large lemon, or 6 dried citrus slices

1 cup extra virgin olive oil

If using fresh fruit, using a razor-sharp vegetable peeler, remove the peel in long strips from the fruit, being careful not to get any of the white pith.

Put the peel or dried slices in a wide-mouthed glass jar, pour in a little of the oil. Muddle with the back of a wooden spoon to release the fragrant citrus oils. Pour in the remaining oil to cover and screw on the lid.

Store the oil in a cool place for a few days before using. It will keep for up to 6 months.

Serve these thin crisps on a cheese board, use as garnish for a cocktail or a bowl of ice cream, or simply enjoy as a snack. It's nice to use a mixture of citrus so you have a colorful selection.

CITRUS CRISPS

6 citrus fruits, each
a different type

1 cup sugar

Preheat the oven to 200°F.

Thinly slice the fruit crosswise and arrange the slices in a single layer on a sheet pan. Sprinkle the sugar evenly over the slices, making sure they are all covered.

Bake the slices for 3 hours. Turn the slices over and continue to bake for 3 to 4 hours longer, until crisp. Transfer the slices to a wire rack in a single layer and leave at room temperature overnight to dry further.

Transfer the slices to an airtight container and store at room temperature for up to 1 month.

This recipe works for all citrus, and it's a great way to use all parts of the fruit so nothing goes to waste. Use the syrup for cocktails, spritzers, ice creams, and sorbets. You can also add rosemary or thyme to the final coating sugar to give the peel an herbal note. Either way, you end up with wonderful candied fruit for baking.

CANDIED PEEL

~Makes about 1 cup

2 navel, Valencia, or other thick-skinned oranges

3 cups sugar, plus more for coating

3 cups water

1/2 teaspoon baking soda

Wash and dry the oranges and cut them into quarters. Using a razor-sharp vegetable peeler, remove the peel, making sure you leave the pith on the peel. Reserve the fruit for another use. Roughly tear the peel into pieces.

Bring a saucepan filled with water to a boil over medium-high heat. Add the peel, reduce the heat to low, and simmer gently for 45 minutes.

Drain the peel and set aside. In the same saucepan, combine the sugar and water and bring to a boil over medium-high heat. Reduce the heat to medium and simmer, stirring occasionally, for about 5 minutes, until the sugar has dissolved completely.

Add the baking soda and stir well. Add the reserved peel, adjust the heat so the syrup is barely simmering, and cook for 45 minutes, until the peel is translucent.

Have ready a wire rack set over a sheet of parchment paper. Using a slotted spoon, remove the peel from the pan, shaking off any excess syrup, and spread it in a single layer on the rack. Let the peel dry at room temperature overnight. The next day, spread some sugar on a sheet pan and roll the peel in the sugar to coat. Store the peel in an airtight container at room temperature for up to 3 months.

This is not really a recipe, but an invitation to make customized frozen ice pops in a dazzling kaleidoscope of colors and tastes. These are also a fun activity for kids. Add fruit or layer them with coconut milk or your favorite yogurt. Or make a grown-up version by lacing the citrus juices with a little vodka or tequila.

STRIPY CITRUS POPS

A selection of freshly squeezed citrus juices, such as:

Blood orange

Yellow, pink, or ruby grapefruit

Orange

Tangerine

Mandarin orange

Lime

Lemon

Pour a layer of juice about 1 inch into frozen pop molds and freeze. Remove the molds from the freezer, pour another citrus juice to the same depth, return the molds to the freezer, and freeze. Continue until you have filled the molds. Keep frozen until ready to eat.

Acknowledgments

We would like to thank: Ten Speed Press; our editors Ali Slagle and Kim Laidlaw for their amazing guidance; Emma Campion and Tatiana Pavlova for the beautiful book design; Hannah Rahill for bringing Citrus to life; Jim Churchill of Churchill Orchard, who gave us great advice and let us roam his groves looking for exquisite Pixies and kishus, among other exotic citrus, for our photos; the Givens family of Mud Creek Ranch in Santa Paula, who offered more varieties of citrus than you can imagine, including the elusive bergamots; Dennis Mitchum for last-minute grapefruits from his garden; Michelle Reiner for her support and wisdom; Luke Sommer for his technical expertise and ability to keep us laughing; Martin, Val's husband, for tasting everything with a smile, and Brett, Victoria's husband, for his support and love.

We loved spending the last year in the world of perfumed citrus—cooking, tasting, and shooting in the studio deep in the citrus groves of Ojai. Our hope is that you can experience that freshness and beauty within our book!

Index

Published in the United States by Ten Speed Press,
an imprint of the Crown Publishing Group, a division of
Penguin Random House LLC, New York.
www.crownpublishing.com
www.tenspeed.com

Ten Speed Press and the Ten Speed Press colophon are
registered trademarks of Penguin Random House LLC.

Library of Congress Cataloging-in-Publication Data
Aikman-Smith, Valerie.
  Citrus : sweet and savory sun-kissed recipes /
Valerie Aikman-Smith and Victoria Pearson.—First Edition.
    pages cm
  Includes bibliographical references and index.
  1. Cooking (Citrus fruits) I. Pearson, Victoria. II. Title.
  TX813.C5A35 2015
  641.6'4304—dc23
                          2015007695

Hardcover ISBN: 978-1-60774-767-3
eBook ISBN: 978-1-60774-768-0

Printed in China

Design by Emma Campion and Tatiana Pavlova

10 9 8 7 6 5 4 3 2 1

First Edition

MEASUREMENT CONVERSION CHARTS

U.S.	IMPERIAL	METRIC
1 tablespoon	½ fl oz	15 ml
2 tablespoons	1 fl oz	30 ml
¼ cup	2 fl oz	60 ml
⅓ cup	3 fl oz	90 ml
½ cup	4 fl oz	120 ml
⅔ cup	5 fl oz (¼ pint)	150 ml
¾ cup	6 fl oz	180 ml
1 cup	8 fl oz (⅓ pint)	240 ml
1¼ cups	10 fl oz (½ pint)	300 ml
2 cups (1 pint)	16 fl oz (⅔ pint)	480 ml
2½ cups	20 fl oz (1 pint)	600 ml
1 quart	32 fl oz (1⅔ pints)	1 l

FAHRENHEIT	CELSIUS/GAS MARK
250°F	120°C/gas mark ½
275°F	135°C/gas mark 1
300°F	150°C/gas mark 2
325°F	160°C/gas mark 3
350°F	175 or 180°C/gas mark 4
375°F	190°C/gas mark 5
400°F	200°C/gas mark 6
425°F	220°C/gas mark 7
450°F	230°C/gas mark 8
475°F	245°C/gas mark 9
500°F	260°C

INCH	METRIC
¼ inch	6 mm
½ inch	1.25 cm
¾ inch	2 cm
1 inch	2.5 cm
6 inches (½ foot)	15 cm
12 inches (1 foot)	30 cm

U.S./IMPERIAL	METRIC
½ oz	15 g
1 oz	30 g
2 oz	60 g
¼ lb	115 g
⅓ lb	150 g
½ lb	225 g
¾ lb	350 g
1 lb	450 g